BLUEGRASS

BLUEGRASS

An Informal Guide

Richard D. Smith

a cappella books

Library of Congress Cataloging-in-Publication Data

Smith, Richard D., 1949–
    Bluegrass: an informal guide / Richard D. Smith
        p.   cm.
    Includes bibliographical references and index.
    ISBN 1-55652-240-1 : $12.95
    1. Bluegrass music—History and criticism.   2. Music appreciation.
ML3520.S65   1995
781.642—dc20   94-49168
                                                         CIP
                                                         MN

© 1995 by Richard D. Smith
All rights reserved
Published by a cappella books
An imprint of Chicago Review Press, Incorporated
814 North Franklin Street, Chicago, Illinois 60610
Printed in the United States of America
5 4 3 2 1

This book is dedicated to Carl Hoffman, who took me into his band, encouraged me, and told me I was a sparkplug; and to Mitch Jayne, who, unlike my schoolteachers, got me to thinking that choosing words and putting them together to tell stories could be lots of fun.

ACKNOWLEDGMENTS

This is not a history of bluegrass as such. That's already been done. Although I've been involved with the music for more than thirty years (the fox of my life is really being chased by the hounds of time!) and although I've been writing and reviewing for bluegrass publications for about half that time, I've still had to lean on a stack of other people's reference material to put this book together. (See Appendix Two for a complete listing).

I'm particularly indebted to (and in awe of) Neil V. Rosenberg, Bob Artis, Robert Cantwell, Bill C. Malone, and Jim Rooney for their seminal books on bluegrass and the history of country music. The work of other writers of books and/or magazine articles has further educated me, either over the years or during specific research for *Bluegrass: An Informal Guide.* They include (but are by no means limited to): Ralph Rinzler, Ivan M. Tribe, Douglas B. Green, Jack Tottle, Eddie Stubbs, Fred Bartenstein, and Bill Vernon.

I'm primarily a mandolin player, so I've needed some help capoing up my insights on other instruments. My discussions of the banjo and the fiddle rely heavily on conversations with Tony Trischka and Kenny Kosek, respectively. I thank them respectfully. Any inaccuracies, errors, or stupid opinions are mine.

Writing about bluegrass has been an integral part of my career as a professional scribbler. So I wish to thank editors who (as Bill Monroe would say) "go a way on back in time": Fred Bartenstein

(*Muleskinner News*), Don Kissil and Marilyn Kochman (*Pickin'*), and Steve Spence (*Bluegrass Unlimited*). Additional thanks to Sharon K. Watts, current managing editor at *Bluegrass Unlimited*, and to Pete Kuykendall, general manager and founder of *BU*, who were both very helpful as I gathered material for this book, who gave me the chance to write for them, and who have always nurtured the many shades of bluegrass with love.

Dan Hays, executive director of the International Bluegrass Music Association, couldn't have been more helpful and gracious during various inquiries. I'm also very grateful to the artists and representatives who provided photos for this book.

Thanks to Bob and Jan Mills for inviting me to the July Fourth party where, during a pause in a jam session, Richard Carlin suggested I write this book. I'm grateful to Linda Matthews of Chicago Review Press for matching Richard's interest.

Finally, other people had a real role: Thanks to the community around Griggstown, New Jersey, for providing the place and situation in which I first played bluegrass; thanks to many people I don't have space to name for being the finest bluegrass-pickin', hangin'-out, sure-you-can-crash-here-tonight-and-sit-up-'til-dawn-talkin'-about-bluegrass friends a man could have; thanks to my mom, Mae W. Smith, the biggest fan of my music and my writing. Finally, thanks to Rose Meyers for her love, hugs, and smiling enthusiasm throughout the project, and her mellowness while the chores took longer to get done because I was peering into the word processor.

CONTENTS

INTRODUCTION

Country music and folk music are experiencing an unprecedented boom. And one of the most beloved and enduring forms of folk-country music is bluegrass: a heartfelt, hard-driving acoustic music first developed in the 1930s by the legendary Bill Monroe.

Bluegrass can be emotionally charged or just plain fun. Frequently it's both. There's a spiritual and almost palpably physical power to this music that goes beyond toe-tapping. Get that banjo driving, fiddle moaning, mandolin chopping, bass booming, and guitar pulsing behind the clear mountain harmonies, and it kind of just saws you off at the knees.

But far from being a hillbillyesque free-for-all, bluegrass is a highly disciplined American art form. Devotees appreciate crisp instrumental playing and tightly structured harmonies from a bluegrass band as highly as classical music audiences value the virtuosity of a top chamber ensemble.

Bluegrass: An Informal Guide is intended to quickly orient the new fan, sharpen his/her ear, and give even life-long devotees additional enjoyment of this wonderfully vital and truly American music.

Bluegrass: An Informal Guide is not a definitive history of the music, however. That's been done by others already, much better than I ever could. The works of these scholar/enthusiasts are listed in Appendix Two under "Resources," and I encourage you

1

to read their books. (After you finish reading mine, of course. Thanks!)

Like other titles in the *Informal Guides* series, this book provides an easy way to get oriented, find out who the major players are, and dive right into the music without wasteful trial and error. If you read about a certain artist and think "Hmmm, that sounds interesting" and buy one of their CDs (or go to one of their shows) and get happy, I'll have been successful.

So how can I do this? Despite the deceptively simple structure of the average bluegrass song, this music is amazingly multifaceted. So I've decided to treat bluegrass like any classical art form.

Just as other musics show definite artistic schools and historical trends (eg., baroque, classical, and romantic music; early, bel canto, romantic, or modern operas), bluegrass can be appreciated in terms of its various styles. Some of these styles are related to persons (Monroe-style; Stanley-style), some are regional (Midwestern-style; California-style), and some reflect other influences (country 'grass; newgrass). So you'll find chapters about the major figures in bluegrass history, about the types of bluegrass that developed in different parts of the country, and about present-day variations on the music that Bill Monroe first developed.

(*Memo to other bluegrass experts*: I know you can quibble with my theories on the grounds that bluegrass performers who became famous in one region of the country often came from somewhere else; within one region people take vastly different approaches to the music; some bands defy easy categorization, etc. etc. I know generalizations often get busted back to privates and creating pigeonholes often results in ruffled feathers and pungent droppings. But I think my approach works.)

Each chapter of *Bluegrass: An Informal Guide* contains suggestions for further listening. Now, friends and neighbors, bluegrass is not completely like classical music. (Yes, you've noticed that.) What I mean is that it doesn't have a body of symphonies and sonatas that get recorded by different people all the time so that no matter what goes out of print there's always a version of Beethoven's Fifth or the Brandenburg Concertos by somebody available somewhere. Bluegrass is more like jazz; it's usually recorded by the people who have written it or otherwise created it. When their records stop selling, they go out of print, and that's that.

Well, that *was* that until the advent of a technological break-through called the compact disc. Now, I'm happy to report, there's huge interest in re-releasing classic bluegrass material on CD. Sometimes these reissues are four-CD set mega-event retro-spectives; expensive, but containing great booklets with detailed biographies of the musicians, rare archival photographs, and complete recording session information.

I've tried to list the best, most representative, and most re-cently released recording by a given artist or band. Now obvi-ously that can't always come together: A great recording might be long out of print and a more recent release might simply not be the artist's best work.

So in a few cases, if I thought a particular recording was pretty darn good but not in print, I've listed it anyway, because 1) the trend to reissues on CD may work its magic by the time you read this; 2) sometimes mail order businesses that specialize in blue-grass have old stuff in their warehouses (especially if you still have one of those funky devices called a record player and don't mind buying those big vinyl platters); 3) used-record shops of-ten have a brisk turnover in good-quality collectibles and you might find something there.

Just as we're living in a happy time of CD reissues, it's also the golden age of bluegrass instructional books, cassettes, and video-tapes. But because of space limitations, all CDs, tapes, records, and videos listed are limited to performance material only. How-ever, the magazines listed in Appendix Two advertise a plethora of instructional material every month.

One potentially unfair situation is that I've mentioned certain good regional bands from the North, Midwest, West, or overseas while equally good or even better southern outfits go uncredited. The problem is that the South is bluegrass music's cradle, and the cradle is endlessly rocking. I admit that a good group from Mon-tana has a better chance of being mentioned than any one of the many good groups from Virginia or Tennessee. If I've left out your favorite band or artist, I do apologize.

A lot of people ask, "How do you define bluegrass?" This is a crucial question, and I talk about it in depth in chapter 1.

In a way bluegrass has become a victim, linguistically, of its own success. The term "bluegrass" is now a household word, broadly applied to any kind of hillbilly music or folk music with a banjo and fiddle. I think that's wrong. I want to show that bluegrass is something more specific.

But people who feel they must protect and defend "traditional" bluegrass define it so narrowly that we throw out the bath water to find a baby is still there but its brother and sister are missing. I'll be applying a broad definition of bluegrass that can embrace jazz- and rock-influenced "newgrass" music on the one hand as well as groups with no banjo but other bluegrass instruments plus recognizable bluegrass timing, harmonies, and song material on the other hand. (In fact, the very first edition of Bill Monroe and His Blue Grass Boys, circa 1939, would fall into the latter category.)

I hope you'll love bluegrass so much that you'll get sawed off at the knees by it and then (after reassembling yourself) want to get involved. If so, jump right in!

There are lots of participation opportunities in bluegrass for an amateur (who, by definition, is someone who loves something); certainly more than you'll find with symphonic music, opera or complex jazz. Check out some of the listings in the resources section; learn to pick and sing; join a bluegrass association; go to a festival and jam in the parking lots and camping areas.

You'll be mighty welcome.

ONE

KNEE DEEP IN THE BLUEGRASS

Going to music shows was high-level entertainment for our family. . . . The first show I remember was Bill Monroe and His Blue Grass Boys on a summer evening in 1946, when I was six years old. Boy, this really *tattooed my brain*. I've never forgotten it: Bill had a real good five-piece band. They took that old hillbilly music, sped it up, and basically invented what is now known as bluegrass music: the bass in its place, the mandolin above it, the guitar tying the two together, and the violin on top, playing the long notes to make it sing. The banjo backed the whole thing up, answering everybody. . . .
That was the end of cowboys and Indians for me. When I got home I held the broom sideward and strutted past the barn, around the pump, and out to the watermelon patch, pretending to play the guitar. I was hooked.
    —Levon Helm of The Band, from *This Wheel's on Fire*, by Levon Helm with Stephen Davis (copyright 1993, Levon Helm and Stephen Davis; used by permission of William Morrow and Company, Inc.)

Bluegrass doesn't make fans, it makes believers.
    —Mitch Jayne of the Dillards

Maybe you first answered the call of hot bluegrass picking and then stayed for its "high lonesome" singing. The excitement of hearing banjo, fiddle, mandolin, and guitar players picking, bowing, and strumming 97 miles per hour around a musical curve while the bass player thumps down a rhythm roadbed just breaks the trail for the close, bluesy harmony singing so spine-tingling it can revive a sunstroke victim (or so I'm told).

And bluegrass puts it all together with vocal and instrumental interplays that provide a disciplined structure for improvisational creativity. Bluegrass is in many respects country music's answer to jazz.

But unlike jazz or country music (or rock or folk for that matter), bluegrass has a definite beginning. It started with a Kentuckian named Bill Monroe who, in 1939, founded a band called the Blue Grass Boys with a mind to creating his own style of music. He did and won a spot on country music's most prestigious showcase, the Grand Ole Opry.

The music would become known as "bluegrass" and be loved around the world. Other musicians would become associated with bluegrass, including Lester Flatt and Earl Scruggs and the Stanley Brothers. It would directly influence the early careers of rock and country stars as prominent as Elvis Presley, Buddy Holly, Jerry Garcia, Marty Stuart, and Ricky Skaggs. Bluegrass would entertain millions when used in the *Beverly Hillbillies* and *Andy Griffith* television shows or on the soundtracks of the movies *Bonnie and Clyde* and *Deliverance.*

Over the years, many people made major contributions to bluegrass. Some even influenced Monroe's own approach to his music. But bluegrass as we know it today began with Bill Monroe, and although he drew heavily on the folk music of the rural South, what he developed was something very new in terms of its structure, harmonies, and even basic tempos.

Some people equate bluegrass with country music. It is a form of country music (it was first played to country music audiences). It has some relation to folk music too. Bluegrass is certainly not the same as the union of commercial country music, cowboy music, and western swing dance music, which became known as "country-and-western." And it's on a different planet from the combination of electric instruments, violin sections, and even vocal chorales known as "the Nashville sound."

Other people equate bluegrass with the "old timer," "mountain," or "hillbilly" modes of southern string band music. Bluegrass has many similarities with these rural cousins but differs in significant ways: Old-time music tends not to have three-finger "Scruggs-style" banjo playing or bass fiddles or tightly arranged harmony singing or jazz-like soloing and improvisation of individual instruments between sung verses.

But more important, old-time music (as the name implies) is much closer to its ancient roots in the Anglo-Scots-Irish music brought over by settlers from the British Isles. Bluegrass, by contrast, is *not* a traditional music. It is actually fairly modern. What is more accurate to say is that bluegrass is a *traditionally-based* music.

There are many shades of bluegrass, from the classic Monroesque mode to the jazz-influenced sounds of "newgrass." But no matter what style becomes your favorite, the distinction between traditional and traditionally-based southern music is important to understand.

But if bluegrass is not the same thing as traditional old-time mountain music, then just what is it?

People have argued long and intensely about what "true" bluegrass is and how to define it. They still do. If you close this book for a moment, you can probably hear them. (No, those are people arguing politics and religion. But it does sound pretty similar sometimes.)

I won't attempt to define bluegrass, certainly not in terms of western music theory. Half of you, not understanding the complex theorems involved, would be confused. The other half of you, most definitely understanding the complex theorems involved, would immediately recognize that I was completely full of black-eyed peas (to use a printable expression).

Instead, I want to offer some characteristics of bluegrass as guidelines. When most of the following elements are present, I think you have bluegrass music. Recognizing these elements will help you get enjoyment out of the music and even enable you to enter the circle of experts without fear of shame.

Ten Basic Characteristics of Bluegrass

1. There are many varieties of bluegrass but they all ultimately derived from the music of Bill Monroe and His Blue Grass Boys.

2. It is an ensemble music. Songs from the bluegrass repertoire might be performed by solo artists, but a band is needed to play bluegrass. That's because there is a need for both lead and rhythm instruments and (usually) harmony singing. (Bluegrass bands usually have four, five, or six members. Under three gets too anemic sounding, and over seven tends to get a bit unwieldy.)

3. It is a string music. Harmonicas and drums are rarely found in bluegrass bands; horns and pianos never.

4. The basic bluegrass instruments are 5-string banjo, fiddle, mandolin, six-string guitar, and bass. Also used at times is resophonic guitar (often referred to as "dobro" guitar, after the most widely used brand) played in a "Hawaiian" slide style. So are additional fiddles or guitars (See "More about the Instruments," next page).

5. Generally, the banjo is the primary instrument with fiddle and/or mandolin in supporting roles. It should be stressed, however, that fiddle was the "soul" of bluegrass before the banjo ever became established as its pumping "heart."

6. As in most types of country music, the offbeat is emphasized in bluegrass (as opposed to blues, rock, and jazz, where the downbeat is usually emphasized).

7. Bluegrass instrumentalists will typically "anticipate" or surge slightly ahead of the beat to give the music extra energy, but not in such a way that the tempo keeps speeding up. (By comparison, blues musicians typically "lay back" behind the main beat to give the music impact and drama, but not in a way that slows or drags down the tempo.) This is an important point: Many people think that the toe-tappin' sound of bluegrass comes from its fast, hoedown-style tempos. But in fact moderately paced bluegrass can still be quite lively if it has that constant surge.

8. Bluegrass vocalists typically perform songs in keys that cause them to sing in higher registers. For male vocalists, this

means that the tenor range is typical for singing bluegrass. (Obviously, women sing bluegrass too; they also tend to pitch it up in their higher ranges.)

9. With the exception of occasional electric bass, the instruments are generally not "electrified": that is, they are not solid-body or semi-acoustic instruments with pickups or built-in microphones. Overall sound system amplification (with microphones for musicians to sing and play into) is an extremely crucial element of live bluegrass performance, however: It makes vocal and instrumental solos audible from the overall ensemble sound, thus giving bluegrass its characteristic dynamics.

   Old-time mountain music, by contrast, features more ensemble unison playing and less soloing, so sound systems are less critical to its performance.

10. Bluegrass has a definite starting point and is therefore not a traditional music (which is why I call it a traditional-style music). But it draws heavily and directly on two major musical traditions: the British-American tradition (Scots-Irish dance tunes and English ballads) plus the African-American tradition (the blues and jazz).

More about the Instruments

[Note to the reader: chapter 15 goes into more detail about individual bluegrass instruments, their histories, their great exponents, and some recommended listening. But here's something for starters.]

BANJO

One definitive statement you can make is that the bluegrass banjo is *always* of the five-string variety and not a four-string "tenor" banjo (just as classical musicians never use standup honky-tonk-style pianos in concert). And unlike many performers of folk or "old-time" banjo music, bluegrass banjoists use instruments with relatively large drums plus resonators and play them loudly. Bluegrass is not a particularly quiet music (in the same way that Mr. Monroe himself, although at times laconic, has never been one to leave a point unmade). That's why large-bodied guitars and flat-backed mandolins are almost universally employed in bluegrass bands: smallbodied guitars and little round-backed mandolins just don't have enough punch to compete with loud banjos and fiddles.

In addition, the bluegrass banjo is always played using a thumb pick and two finger picks. Bluegrass banjo players might know how to use the old-time pick-brush style known as "frailing" and might even know how to use a plectrum, but if they're picking bluegrass, they're doing it in some variation of a three-finger style.

The banjo picking of Earl Scruggs was showcased in the Blue Grass Boys in the mid-1940s, his syncopated approach to the instrument becoming so popular that three-finger bluegrass banjo picking is generically called "Scruggs style." It's almost unheard of now to have a bluegrass band without a banjo. But it's not impossible. Monroe had only fiddle, mandolin, guitar, and bass in his 1939 band, which easily qualifies as a true bluegrass group.

FIDDLE

Bluegrass's most direct link with its Scots-Irish roots is the fiddle. Many dance tunes traditionally played on the fiddle (such as "Bill Cheatum," "Sallie Goodin," "Soldier's Joy," and "Devil's Dream") have become standards in the bluegrass repertoire. Bluegrass fiddling differs significantly from its "old-time" forebears, however: bow strokes are usually longer, and there is more use of "bluesy" sliding up into notes and/or use of "double stops" (pushing down on the strings to create two-note "chords" instead of playing the strings open), all of which represent some debt to the technique of the "western swing" musicians many early bluegrass fiddlers admired. Although old-time music and bluegrass sometimes use two fiddles in one band, "twin fiddling" in bluegrass entails not unison playing but tightly arranged harmony.

MANDOLIN

This was Mr. Monroe's instrument, for which he created a dual role. When not playing lead solos, it's strummed as a rhythm instrument. This "rhythm chop" comes on the offbeat, giving the mandolin the function of a snare drum in the band and also giving bluegrass more of its distinctive sound. Although a mandolin may be used to introduce or "kick off" songs, it often later plays variations on the melodies first stated by the banjo and fiddle. Because Monroe as a young man loved both square dance fiddling and blues guitar playing, he incorporated elements of both in creating his seminal mandolin technique.

GUITAR

Bluegrass guitarists are primarily rhythm players, but today many are adept at contributing solos. Thanks to the talents of such musicians as Doc Watson and Tony Rice, the role for guitar as a lead bluegrass instrument is expanding.

Unlike folk blues guitarists, bluegrass guitarists generally use a flatpick (plectrum). There are a few fingerpickers in bluegrass, however. In the early days, many singer/guitarists played rhythm using a thumb and a fingerpick. (This school included Clyde Moody, Carter Stanley, Lester Flatt, and Bill Monroe's brother Charlie. Flatt's use of fingerpicks to produce a full, facile rhythm has never been equaled and may now be a lost art.)

Electric guitars are virtually never used in bluegrass. Part of this is ideological—"Bill Monroe never used one." (Actually Monroe did agree to a recording session with a country-western backup trio of drums, electric guitar, and electric bass. He was displeased with the results and never repeated the experiment.) But there are sound reasons (pun intended) for this. Electric and acoustic instruments don't combine easily to produce a pleasingly balanced band sound.

While we're on the subject, one caveat about the "electronically amplified" guitars, banjos, fiddles, etc. you may see in concert these days. Despite the wires dripping off them, many are actually acoustic instruments with tiny microphones mounted on them. In other words, the microphone has just been made small and mounted on the instrument instead of being a big mike on a stand in front of the performer.

BASS

Many bands prefer a bass of the standup, acoustic variety and of the size known in orchestral music as a "three quarter bass" (although if you've ever tried to get one out of a car and lug it through the seemingly endless grounds of an outdoor festival to the stage under a hot summer sun, you'll won't think of it as anything other than the giant uneconomical size). Bands often find that an acoustic bass has a more pleasing "traditional" sound than an electric bass with a guitar-style body. I've noticed there's just something in the way a standup bass is constructed that causes its playing to complement the surging bluegrass offbeat, while a downbeat played on an electric bass tends to drag the time down. Or maybe most electric bass players start with rock-n-roll and aren't used to clipped country rhythms.

DOBRO

This is the brand name for the most popular make of resophonic guitar (an acoustic instrument with built-in pie pan–shaped resonators). Typically played "Hawaiian" style with a slide instead of being fretted like a regular guitar, the dobro was popularized in bluegrass by Josh Graves while playing with Lester Flatt, Earl Scruggs, and the Foggy Mountain Boys. Flatt and Scruggs completely replaced the mandolin with the dobro in their band's later years. Not surprisingly, Bill Monroe has never used a resophonic guitar in the Blue Grass Boys, but in many bands the dobro and mandolin complement each other.

DRUMS

Sometimes used in recording sessions, drums are very rarely used in concert. With the snare-like offbeat of the mandolin, much of the need for drums is taken care of.

MISCELLANEOUS INSTRUMENTS

As noted earlier, the piano is not a bluegrass band instrument (although it has been used on rare occasions in recording sessions). However, an early ancestor of the piano, the hammered dulcimer, is now being used in bluegrass contexts to play traditional-style tunes.

Harmonicas are also rarely used. The blown-reed sound of the harmonica doesn't always mix well with such stringed instruments as banjo, fiddle, and mandolin. And unfortunately the harmonica has gotten a lousy reputation in bluegrass circles because of players who are not aware of the bluegrass format of trading solos in jazz-style exchanges. Some harmonica players make themselves obnoxious by entering jam sessions in bluegrass festival parking lots and just wailing away non-stop over everyone else, rarely coming close to the melody line. But in the right hands, the harmonica has made a beautiful, bluesy contribution to the basic "lonesome" bluegrass sound.

Rhythm instruments such as spoons, jaw harps, and washboards are never found in a bluegrass context except as novelties (or uninvited jam session nuisances). Bluegrass is not jug-band music, and anyway these instruments are not suited to the surging tempos that give bluegrass its energy.

Now that we've characterized bluegrass, seen how it differs from similar folk and country musics, and gotten an idea of its finer artistic points, it's time to wade deeper into the bluegrass: How it was created, where, when, and by whom; what makes different styles unique; and why bluegrass gives us chills and just plain keeps sawing us off at the knees.

TWO

THE PREFACE AS CHAPTER AND VERSE
Bill Monroe

An institution is the lengthened shadow of one man.
—**Ralph Waldo Emerson, American essayist and poet**

Bluegrass has been defined by the character and artistic sensibilities of one man: Bill Monroe, a proud and intense native of the Bluegrass State of Kentucky. As a young man, he listened as others did to the music around him—Scots-Irish dance tunes, English ballads, African-American blues, the hymns and harmonies of church. Then he put them together in a new way.

Many people have given color to the many shades of bluegrass today. But had Monroe not lived, it's doubtful the music would exist as we know it.

We can only speculate how the personality of a Johann Sebastian Bach influenced baroque music. But we have a good idea of how the personality of Bill Monroe defined bluegrass, so it's worth looking at his life closely.

1. Bill Monroe, the Father of Bluegrass (courtesy of Buddy Lee Attractions).

The Child Is Father to the Man

William Smith Monroe was born on Jerusalem Ridge near Rosine, Kentucky, on Friday the 13th of September 1911. Far from finding this a bad omen, he later quipped that he was "lucky from Kentucky." He was the son of James Buchanan "Buck" Monroe (believed to be a descendant of President James Monroe) and Malissa A. Monroe. His father was nearly 54 when he was born, his mother 41. Perhaps this created the affinity Bill felt with things that, as he put it, "go a way on back in time": Buck, born in 1857, would have remembered the Civil War.

Bill was the youngest of ten children. Later, when the musical Monroe sons took over the family instruments, older brother Birch got the prized fiddle, Charlie the guitar, and Bill was left with the mandolin. Reportedly, his siblings insisted at one point that he string it with only four strings and not the full four sets of double strings so he wouldn't "make too much noise." Bill's desire to prove himself was formed in these years.

From his father, who raised crops, mined coal, and cut timber on his six-hundred-acre farm, Bill learned a work ethic that would stand him in good stead the rest of his life. From his red-haired mother, who played the accordion or fiddle in her few free moments, he inherited a love of music.

Bill eventually learned to play the guitar, but it was on the mandolin that he shone. He developed a revolutionary style of mandolin playing: not the sweet silvery tinklings and sustained tremolos that drifted from the parlors of late-nineteenth-century American homes but a powerful combination of fiddle and guitar styles capable of handling fast breakdowns and dramatic ballads with equal ease.

On the mandolin, Bill reproduced the rhythmic fiddle bowing of his mother's brother, Pendleton Vandiver, a local trader and laborer whom Bill immortalized years later in his song "Uncle Pen." Monroe has claimed that Pen had "the prettiest shuffle on the bow you ever saw" and an impeccable rhythm sense that kept him in great demand at local dances.

Although Monroe played with a flatpick, he also incorporated the staccato elements of the blues-guitar finger picking of Arnold

Schultz, an African-American railroad worker who befriended
young Bill and whose playing greatly influenced many other
guitarists in the region (and beyond—Schultz is now believed to
have influenced a regional style of finger picking practiced by
such guitarists as Ike Everly, father of the 1950s pop stars the
Everly Brothers; Merle Travis, and Chet Atkins).

"I've always wanted to have some blues in my music," Monroe has said, and the pervasive use of blues greatly differentiates
bluegrass from many other forms of folk and country music.
Monroe has long acknowledged his debt to and respect for
African-American musicians.

The Monroes were good church-goers and young Bill learned
much about harmony singing from the services. He never
learned to read music. (His eyes were crossed as a youth and he
could not take advantage of the "singing schools" held periodically in mountain communities that taught youngsters the rudi-
ments of music theory.) But he held in his mind every tone, tim-
bre, slide, and shuffle of his compositions and taught them to his
fiddle players through a combination of playing them on his
mandolin, singing certain passages, and using body language
until the fiddle reproduced just what Monroe heard in his mind.

Bill's crossed eyes not only affected his vision but made him
the butt of teasing and cheap jokes. The boy's feelings were so often hurt that when strangers came near the family farm (which
was on the main wagon road to Rosine) he would hide in the
barn until they were gone. Later he had a successful operation to
straighten his eyes. But no medical procedure could remove the
loneliness that had crossed the soul of the lad, teased by
strangers and lorded over by his older brothers and sisters.

Such experiences were doubtless the start of feelings of sorrow
and isolation that would later be given such powerful expression
in the "high lonesome" sound of bluegrass—and that would
strike empathetic chords in the souls of millions.

Portrait of the Artist as a Strong Young Man

Bill's mother died in 1921 when he was ten. About three years
later, his brothers left home to seek work in northern factories

and refineries. In 1928, his father died. (Bill would later use the respective inscriptions on their tombstones—"Gone but not forgotten" and "We will meet again"—to write the chorus of "Memories of Mother and Dad.") After a period of "baching it" with his Uncle Pen, he left Kentucky in 1929 to join thousands of other southerners who had headed north to find work.

He got a job at the Sinclair refinery in Whiting, Indiana, and during the depths of the Depression was the sole support of his brothers Birch and Charlie and other relatives living in the area. Monroe thrived on hard work here as he had on the farm, describing himself in these days as "a stout fellow." (Once, on a lark, he gathered up the members of his band—one on his shoulders, one on his back, and one in either arm—supporting their weight and his, a total of 960 pounds.)

Naturally, the brothers played music whenever they could, and with all the southerners in the industrialized cities who craved the sounds of home, they had ample opportunities. They performed with their girlfriends as part of a performing square dance team. Bill and Charlie turned professional (Birch would later perform with Bill in the 1940s as a bass-playing and singing member of the Blue Grass Boys), leaving the Chicago area about 1934 for tremendous success on major radio stations, at live shows throughout the Midwest and South, and (starting in 1936) on record as the Monroe Brothers (see "Bluegrass Brothers" and "Bluegrass Cousins" in Appendix One).

A striking pair they were, two big, solid, handsome men, impeccably dressed in suits and Stetsons. Lester Flatt used to recall the Monroe Brothers "cutting a path walking down a street like a hot knife through butter." They were far from the image of the tattered, bearded, jug-toting hillbilly and far also from the sequined pseudo-cowboy stars who came later. When Monroe had a band of his own, he dressed them in "jodphur" riding pants, riding boots, dress shirts, ties, and Stetsons. More recent editions of the Blue Grass Boys have worn sports jackets or even suits, the clothes proclaiming the dignity and authority that differentiates bluegrass from much of the old-time and country-and-western music with which it is often confused.

Charlie was in many ways a jovial overgrown kid in comparison to Bill who (although possessed of a merry sense of humor) usually faced the world with the serious demeanor associated with his Scots ancestors. Both had forceful personalities expressed through their music. And occasionally through their fists: Neither brother was a stranger to the violence typical of life in both the isolated mountains and the crowded factory yards. Bluegrass today has its share of songs of crime and mayhem (see "Crime and Punishment, Bluegrass Style"). While it does not cultivate the tough Harley-riding, honky-tonk-brawling image of some country musicians, bluegrass was clearly created by men who were not shrinking violets.

Bill established himself with his scorching mandolin style and strong tenor harmonies (which were almost like independent melody lines), and he probably chafed under the position of leadership assumed by Charlie, who was eight years his senior. In 1938, the Monroe Brothers broke up.

The Bluegrass Sound Is Born

At first, Charlie kept working with mandolinist/tenors as part of a duet. But Bill had a band sound in mind. The major elements would come from the Monroe Brothers' music: high tenor harmony, guitar bass runs, driving mandolin, and songs that hearkened back to the traditional music of the Appalachians and mid-South. The repertoire was satisfying for personal reasons—the musicians genuinely loved performing the old songs—but it was important for commercial reasons, too. The country music industry was growing as transplanted southerners in big cities yearned for home and were delighted by music that reinforced their cultural identities.

Bill first founded a group called the Kentuckians. Unfortunately it was never recorded, but it was apparently an interesting quartet of mandolin, fiddle, and guitar, plus a jug player. Then in 1939, Bill founded the Blue Grass Boys band, rehearsed them until he got the sound he wanted, then auditioned for the Grand Ole Opry, a popular country music show broadcast live on Saturday nights on WSM radio, whose powerful "clear channel" station was heard in many parts of the nation.

For the audition, Monroe's band played the rousing fiddle tune "Katy Hill" and an uptempo version of "The Muleskinner Blues," a 1920s hit by Jimmie Rodgers (the "Yodeling Brakeman" and country music's first true superstar—see Appendix One). "Muleskinner" became his signature song. Perhaps Monroe's pride and work ethic responded to the song of a teamster who brags about his prowess in rousting even the most recalcitrant animal on a wagon team. But there was more to it. Much more.

Monroe not only speeded up Rodgers' song from its original tempo. He put in a surging beat, a compelling anticipation in the rhythm that lifted the listener—and won Bill a spot on the Opry. " 'The Muleskinner Blues' was important because it established the timing for bluegrass music," Monroe once told me. Indeed, the timing was so important that at first Monroe played guitar so that the opening run would have just the tempo and attack he wanted. (In later years, Monroe played the opening on mandolin, followed by a guitar run, then by a full fiddle solo.)

Monroe made a number of other conscious decisions in shaping his music. Because he had primarily sung high tenor harmonies to Charlie's second tenor or baritone range leads, Bill knew his greatest strength lay in the higher range. So he pitched his solo vocals in higher keys than they would normally be sung by other country and folk performers because it suited his voice better.

For example, many folk musicians sing "Little Maggie" in G. Monroe sings it in B. He would sometimes embellish vocals with shifts into falsetto—particularly in the yodeling numbers that were popular in the 1930s and '40s—that were like a race car driver shifting gears and suddenly wheeling away. These higher-than-normal keys not only suited Monroe's voice, they gave his music an edge like a well-honed knife. Of course, Monroe was not the first to pitch his voice so high (other Appalachian singers did it), but it became his influential hallmark.

All this was pretty radical for its time. Unlike jazz, where musicians routinely transpose keys to suit vocalists, many folk and mountain music instrumentalists played for convenience in keys that allowed the use of a number of "open" strings. (For example, the strings of the fiddle and its cousin the mandolin are tuned from high to low E-A-D-G. Playing in the key of A gives the option of sounding the untouched E, A, and D strings because the primary chords of the key of A are A, D, and E. Neat, clean, easy, and above all safe. The key of B-flat, with its primary chords B-flat, D-sharp, and F, offers few "open" strings.) All this is less of a problem for banjo and guitar players, who can put capos—special string clamps—on their instruments that raise the pitches of their strings uniformly so they can use familiar fingerings in different keys. But fiddlers, mandolinists, and bass players knew it would require work to fulfill Monroe's edict that an instrumentalist should "play it where you sing it."

Just how he sang was awe-inspiring. One musical analysis of bluegrass singing (by Mayne Smith in "An Introduction to Bluegrass," *Journal of American Folklore* Vol. 78, 1965, pp. 245–256) shows how amazingly complex it really is: anticipations, passing tones, and ornamental slides create dissonances; flatted pitches, rising attacks, falling releases, and grace notes provide other ornamentation. The bluesy shifts from minor to major thirds are a particular trademark of Monroe's vocal music.

Trio harmonies usually consist of a tenor sung a third above the lead line and a baritone sung a fifth below, but occasionally (as in Monroe's stunning "When the Golden Leaves Begin to Fall") over the lead in the chorus will be a tenor but over that will be a "high baritone" line a fifth above the lead.

The higher "bluegrass" keys had another effect. The acoustic instruments being used for bluegrass—fiddle, mandolin, guitar and in particular the 5-string banjo added in the 1940s—seemed to cut through the air. They just sounded livelier.

I used to play in a band with an ace banjo picker named Dave Magram. When the key of B was announced for a song, he would put his capo on and smile somewhat demonically, saying, "B for Bluegrass!" He knew his Gibson RB-4 Mastertone was going to crack like a whip in that key. Actually, many aspiring pickers still don't know the value of getting "keyed up." Bluegrass banjos are usually tuned to an open G-chord and G is a common key for folk songs, so many people just grab themselves a fistful of G without seeing if the song would sound better sung in A, B-flat, or B. There's no point in straining your voice beyond its range, but higher pitches put a distinctive edge on bluegrass vocals. That's why, although Johnny Cash has been a friend to bluegrass, the music has very few low-voiced Johnny Cash–style singers. It's another important way bluegrass differs from much of country music.

Monroe experimented with his sound. He gained confidence in his songwriting, including more and more original material. Around 1942 he even added an accordion to his band. And about the same time, he became intrigued by the sound of the finger-picked 5-string banjo and hired a couple of players.

In 1945 it all came together. Monroe had a smooth-voiced guitarist named Lester Flatt and the two blended very well. Then a young 5-string banjo wizard from North Carolina named Earl Scruggs auditioned and was immediately hired. History was about to be made.

Scruggs was well on his way to perfecting a three-finger style of banjo picking. There were many fine old-timey players who used thumb-and-forefinger picking or who "frailed" in a finger-tip-strumming style. But there was a school of North Carolina players who used versatile three-finger (thumb, index, middle) patterns or "rolls" that brought out an incredible sound in the banjo. For every melody note there were several accompanying rhythm notes, often presented in syncopation. Best of all, the melody always stood out in this shower of music.

DeWitt "Snuffy" Jenkins and other North Carolinians had been creating a new voice for the banjo in addition to its role as an accompaniment for fiddle, the singing of mountain airs, or the delivery of minstrel entertainment. Earl Scruggs was not the first man to three-finger pick a banjo, but he had developed an incredibly fluid style that amazed Monroe and other Opry performers.

Audiences loved this revolutionary banjo sound and Monroe began featuring it. Opry master of ceremonies George D. Hay (aka "The Solemn Old Judge") introduced the band with "Here's Bill Monroe and His Blue Grass Boys and Earl with his fancy banjo."

With the addition of Scruggs' banjo to Flatt's rich lead vocals, Monroe's powerful tenor and mandolin, and the passionate, bluesy fiddling of Chubby Wise, the bluegrass sound was fully defined. "Will You Be Loving Another Man?" "Bluegrass Breakdown," "Little Cabin Home on the Hill," and other compositions from this period have become central to nearly every bluegrass band's repertoire. The licks, riffs, and vocal inflections used by these musicians constitute every bluegrasser's musical vocabulary. The 1945–46 Blue Grass Boys set the standard for every bluegrass band that ever after put pick to string.

Bluegrass and Jazz

Monroe was of course not a pioneer in everything he did. The Cumberland Ridge Runners featuring Karl Davis and Harty Taylor had 5-string banjo, fiddle, mandolin, guitar, and standup bass instrumentation before bluegrass; Charlie Poole and the North Carolina Ramblers featured both banjo picking and dark-suited seriousness in the 1920s.

But bluegrass was modernized old-time music with real jazz influences. As Cantwell and other country music scholars have pointed out, jazz was very popular in Chicago when Monroe began performing on WLS radio there, and it was jazz of a type that featured instrumentalists coming forth from the texture of the orchestra to solo and also to improvise. (Proof that Monroe was listening to this kind of jazz lies in the fact that his mandolin instrumental "Milenberg Joy" is a reworking of "Milneburg Joy," a Jelly Roll Morton composition recorded in 1923 by the New Orleans Rhythm Kings with Morton and Louis Armstrong.)

Indeed, when folklorist Alan Lomax helped bring bluegrass national notice in a 1959 *Esquire* magazine article, he called a bluegrass band "a sort of mountain Dixieland combo." Lomax compared the banjo to a hot clarinet, the mandolin passages to trumpet bursts, and the fiddle bowing to trombone sliding, with the guitar and bass, of course, being a rhythm section.

But bluegrass musicians couldn't just stand up as jazz horn players did in those days: the microphone became a vital part of bluegrass to allow solos and the lead voice to stand out from the instrumental context. (Traditionalists please note that bluegrass has been "electrified" in this sense since day one.) On stage choreography—"working the mike"—and gathering tightly around a single mike to sing harmony—"working close"—became an exciting visual art. With today's rock-style sound systems providing separate vocal and instrumental mikes for each and every musician, such motion-filled performances are all but gone, although admittedly the sound is clearer.

Jazz also influenced the banjo: "Bugle Call Rag" and "Farewell Blues," which received memorable treatments from Flatt and Scruggs, were originally big band numbers. Scruggs' solos on the 12-bar bluesy "Bluegrass Special" and "Foggy Mountain Special" owe much to jazz-band influences. The genius of Scruggs, Monroe, and others was how they incorporated the sounds of jazz and blues into their special music.

I once asked Monroe if it were true that he could have developed other styles of music besides the bluegrass we know today. He said that was true. When asked what they would have been, he smiled, looked uncharacteristically embarrassed, and said, "I wouldn't want to mention them!" But listen to his swinging version of "Rocky Road Blues," circa 1942, or his 1957 recordings of "Breaking in a Brand New Pair of Shoes" and "Sally-Jo," the latter featuring a hot guitar introduction by Cajun musician Doug Kershaw, and you may hear what might have been.

Why They Called It "Rockabilly": Rock-n-Roll's Bluegrass Roots

One evening in 1954, a former member of the Louisiana Hayride country music show named Elvis Presley was in Nashville for a guest appearance on the Grand Ole Opry. Backstage, he sought out Bill Monroe to offer an apology.

In a high-spirited jam at the Sun recording studios in Memphis, Presley, lead guitarist Scotty Moore, and bassist Bill Black had turned Monroe's stately waltz "Blue Moon of Kentucky" into an uptempo rocker. Producer and Sun company owner Sam Phillips recorded their version and from the control room exulted, "That's fine. Hell, that's different. That's a pop song now, nearly 'bout." (Elvis Presley, The Sun Session CD, RCA Victor 6414-2-R.) It was not only a pop song, it was a hit, Presley's first.

Monroe, however, was not offended by the liberties taken with his song. "If it helps your career, I'm for it 100 percent," he said. Monroe later re-recorded the piece, the first half in 3/4 time, the second half in 4/4 a la Presley. (The original "Blue Moon of Kentucky" is available on The Essential Bill Monroe and His Blue Grass Boys, 1945–1949, Columbia/Legacy (Sony) C2K-52478, Monroe's remake on Bill Monroe and His Blue Grass Boys, 1950–1958, Bear Family Records BCD 15529.)

Meanwhile, a young Texan named Buddy Holly also stood on the brink of early rock-n-roll fame. Holly, who had formed a bluegrass band as a teenager, later said that the falsetto yodels and driving, strumming guitar solo on his smash rock hit "Peggy Sue" were directly patterned after Monroe's high tenor singing and mandolin playing (compare Holly's "Peggy Sue" guitar break (Buddy Holly: From the Original Master Tapes, MCA MCAD-5540) with Monroe's mandolin on his recording of "Bluegrass Breakdown."

Early Bluegrass was lumped in with the traditional-style country musics known collectively as "Hillbilly." Many early white rockers had played this music, hence the term "Rockabilly" for country-influenced rock-n-roll. Listen to Elvis Presley, Carl Perkins, Jerry Lee Lewis, and Johnny Cash rendering such Monroe classics as "Little Cabin Home on the Hill," "Summertime Is Past and Gone," "I Hear a Sweet Voice Calling," and "Sweetheart, You Done Me Wrong" during a 1956 jam session at the Sun Record studios in Memphis, captured on The Million Dollar Quartet (RCA 2023-4-R). Some bluegrass lead vocalists crossed over into rockabilly in the 1950s (Mac Wiseman, Teenage Hangout, Bear Family 15694).

The Monroe/bluegrass influence on early rock-n-roll went further. The duet singing of the Monroe Brothers influenced a generation of popular country acts, notably the Louvin Brothers, the Delmore Brothers, and the Blue Sky Boys, whose singing shaped the music of Don and Phil Everly. The Beatles, in turn, were directly influenced by the Everly Brothers and Buddy Holly.

Bill Monroe, the Father of Bluegrass and also the Granddaddy of Rock-n-Roll? Well, a great-uncle at least.

The Later Years: Sorrows and Vindication

Monroe, although gracious to his fans, had always been something of a loner, and in the 1950s he became even more taciturn, developing a harder edged, even more intensely personal music that further defined the "high lonesome" sound. A tempestuous personal life led him to pen some of his most moving "true" songs ("On and On," "Memories of You," "Used To Be"). Some of the angers and sorrows of his early days seemed to come back to bedevil him, and although he did not respond by drowning his sorrows (he has never smoked nor drank), he seems to have demonstrated signs of what modern psychologists call "a wounded inner child." Indeed, Monroe recorded a series of poignant songs whose protagonists are dying or abandoned children ("I Hear a Sweet Voice Calling," "Put My Little Shoes Away," "The Little Girl and the Dreadful Snake," and "Left Out on the Street").

It must also have been a disappointing time for a man not yet at the peak of his creativity who should, in theory, be reaching wider and wider audiences. But rock music had rolled over the nation and crushed interest in acoustic folk and country music almost to splinters. This was pretty ironic, considering the influence that Monroe's music had on early "rockabillies." What was left of the market for bluegrass was largely taken over by his hugely successful former employees, Lester Flatt and Earl Scruggs. Until hindsight showed that imitation had been the sincerest form of flattery, Monroe was understandably embittered by the feeling that the music he created had been co-opted. Except for his loyal fans and continued appearances on the Opry, Monroe had become something of a footnote to country music history.

But Bill Monroe's best years on earth were ahead of him. In the 1960s, largely through the efforts of folklorist (and later manager) Ralph Rinzler, Monroe was recognized as the true father of bluegrass and welcomed as a great folk artist by folk music revival audiences. In 1965 country music promoter Carleton Haney produced the first all-bluegrass music festival weekends (with the help of Rinzler and inspired by an earlier one-day success staged by Bill Clifton), opening up a whole new world for bluegrass fans.

Monroe attracted musicians who helped him reach new heights: banjoists Bill Keith (who had perfected a method of fretting and picking that allowed banjo players to play complicated straight melody lines such as those in fiddle tunes) and Lamar Grier; guitarist/vocalists Del McCoury, Peter Rowan, and son James Monroe; fiddlers Richard Greene, Byron Berline, and

Kenny Baker (who returned for a long stay and recorded an album of Uncle Pen's fiddle tunes, a long-cherished Monroe project he had "been holding back for just the right fiddler").

Monroe was a living legend of country music and the stars of Nashville music, which for a time had treated bluegrass like a poor relative, clamored to record with him. Monroe found time to stay healthy by working on his farm in Goodlettsville, Tennessee, and he aged well, bouncing back quickly from a bout with cancer and from a broken hip.

In retrospect, one of his greatest triumphs came on the evening of July 19, 1994, at the old Ryman Auditorium. The building had been home to the Grand Ole Opry longer than any other site, but when the Opry moved out to its "Opryland" complex in the 1980s some feared that the Ryman would one day be torn down.

Instead, it was refurbished and was put to use in a series of Tuesday night bluegrass shows sponsored by Martha White Flour (a company long associated with the careers of Flatt and Scruggs and other bluegrass bands). Heading the bill on opening night was, of course, Bill Monroe.

There was a huge surprise for the audience as time turned back nearly 50 years: Monroe was joined on stage by Earl Scruggs and veteran fiddler Benny Sims to recreate the sound of the 1945 ensemble that had defined the bluegrass sound forever. Taking the place of the late Lester Flatt on guitar and vocals was Ricky Skaggs, a country music star who has stayed close to his bluegrass roots, and ace session bassist Roy Husky, Jr.

The Ryman reverberated once more to "Little Cabin Home on the Hill," "Bluegrass Breakdown," and "Roll in My Sweet Baby's Arms" by the men who made them classics. After years of joy and heartache, boom, bust, and renewal, Bill Monroe and his music—like the Ryman itself—had remained firm and beloved.

Even better, the bitterness of the past had been healed. "I'm glad that we're all friends with each other," said Monroe.

And yes, the show was recorded. By the time you read this, it will probably have been released on its own or as a Ricky Skaggs-and-friends disc—part of the legacy of the remarkable man from Jerusalem Ridge, Kentucky.

Kenny Baker. *Kenny Baker Plays Bill Monroe*, County 761 (Monroe's longtime fiddler; featuring Monroe on mandolin)

Bill Monroe and His Blue Grass Boys. *Muleskinner Blues*, RCA 2494

———. *The Essential Bill Monroe and His Blue Grass Boys, 1945–1949*. Columbia/Legacy (Sony) C2K-52478

———. *Bluegrass 1959–1969*, Bear Family 15529

———. *Bluegrass 1970–1979*, Bear Family 15606

———. *In The Pines*, County CCS-114

———. *Bill Monroe's Uncle Pen*, Decca/MCA 75348

———. *Country Music Hall of Fame*, MCA 10082

———. *Bill Monroe and Friends*, MCA 949 (duets with Nashville country music stars)

———. *Live at the Opry*, MCA 42286

———. *Off the Record*, Smithsonian/Folkways 40063 (rare live band tracks from 1956 to 1969)

———. *Bill Monroe from 1936 to 1994*, MCA 11048 (includes Monroe Brothers recordings)

Bill Monroe and James Monroe. *Father and Son*, MCA 310

Bill Monroe and Doc Watson. *Live Duet Recordings*, Smithsonian/Folkways 40064 (rare recordings with Monroe and the flatpicking guitarist and traditional singer)

THREE

WAY UP ON THE FOGGY MOUNTAIN TOP

Flatt and Scruggs

One day I was listening to Roy Queen's program up there in St. Louis, and they had a new group. . . . It was Lester Flatt and Earl Scruggs. . . . and then Queen said they were going to be at the Chain of Rocks Park in St. Louis, and I went up there . . . and boy—I'll tell you what—I stood right in the front row with my mouth open, and I think it had a profound effect on me, 'cause I've never been right since. . . .
   —John Hartford to interviewer Doug Green

Monroe's compelling sound inspired imitators and competitors in the 1940s and '50s who went on to become members of the "traditional" bluegrass pantheon. Many of these started in the Monroe mode but quickly developed their own individual and immediately recognizable sounds.

Indeed, some had been trained by Monroe himself.

The most successful of Monroe's rivals proved to be his former employees Flatt and Scruggs. Lester's genial MC work and vocal stylings perfectly showcased Earl's stellar banjo work. So influential was Earl's perfection of North Carolina–style synco-

31

pated three-finger playing that bluegrass banjo playing became generically known as "Scruggs picking" (see "Banjo" in chapter 15).

Monroe had had two other banjo players: David Akeman, whose comedy persona was "Stringbean, the Kentucky Wonder," and Jim Andrews, a tenor banjo player and also a comedian. Flatt was initially pained that Monroe intended to audition another banjo player. Perhaps he had had enough of banjo-picking comics, but he also felt that their technique was just not up to the swift tempos the Blue Grass Boys were capable of playing.

But as we've seen, Earl Scruggs was up to those tempos and more. Although he had not yet perfected the full range of techniques that would soon make him the master of the Mastertone, he had his basic right-hand "roll" and a crisp sound. (But Uncle Dave Macon, the rollicking banjoist who was one of the Opry's first big stars, just couldn't relate to a non-comedian banjo picker. Macon, who called Earl "Ernest," used to say, "You ain't funny a lick, Ernest.")

Flatt and Scruggs stayed with Monroe about four years, leaving within weeks of each other in 1948. Life on the road was demanding to say the least. The band toured widely, worked nearly every day of the week, sometimes did two shows a day, and literally would not see a bed for days at a time. One Blue Grass Boy later claimed that space was a precious commodity in Monroe's "Bluegrass Special" touring limo; no room to stretch out while you slept, no room even to put your Stetson and expect it to remain uncrushed. Therefore you slept sitting up, wearing your hat!

No wonder early bluegrass has such a lean, mean, impassioned sound. Lester and Earl tired of the lifestyle. Scruggs briefly returned to work at a North Carolina cotton mill. But some informal living-room picking sessions soon convinced the young men to try it again, this time as their own bosses. The band of Lester Flatt, Earl Scruggs, and the Foggy Mountain Boys was born, and it went on to become probably the biggest phenomenon in bluegrass history.

What made the Foggy Mountain Boys so great? The band had nearly perfect chemistry and combination of talents from the very start. Earl Scruggs had a sense-shaking banjo style, writing the book on three-finger picking with every right-hand roll and fretting variation up the neck. So powerful was his impact that future banjo master Sonny Osborne well remembers being a child and hearing Scruggs in person for the first time in a basement radio studio. Young Sonny hid behind a large supporting column in the room because the experience was overwhelming.

Lester Flatt not only had a mellow voice but also delivered lyrics with deceptively easy timing matched by his fluid guitar strumming. Scruggs played backup banjo that was not merely excellent but on occasion absolutely perfect. For an example of how all these elements could come together, listen to their classic recording of "Doin' My Time." On stage, Flatt tied it all together with his friendly MC work.

More needs to be said about Flatt's grossly undervalued rhythm guitar playing. Listen to it closely. Like many other guitarists of his generation (including Charlie Monroe, Clyde Moody, and Carter Stanley), and unlike the hot flatpickers of today, Flatt used a thumb pick plus a single fingerpick on his forefinger. He would hit a bass string with his thumb on the downbeat, then simultaneously brush down with his thumb and pick up with his forefinger on the upbeat. On fast numbers, he could drag his thumb down across the lower four strings of the guitar, creating a run from a low G to middle G (a technique now popularly known as the "Lester Flatt G Run," although such mountain guitarists as Riley Puckett and Maybelle Carter had used similar runs before). Flatt could also hammer from D/E to open G string with perfect timing.

Flatt's combination of solid and perfectly executed bass runs and what can only be described as a pinch/strum rhythm has never been equaled—nor even approached, as his partner's banjo picking has. I would venture to say that the true Lester Flatt rhythm guitar style is today a lost art.

The Foggy Mountain Boys were a band of considerable subtlety. Take their original recording of "Foggy Mountain Breakdown" (which would again soar to popularity years later on the soundtrack of the movie *Bonnie and Clyde*). Earl definitely plays an E-minor on the banjo and the bass further reinforces this by

walking down from G to E. But Lester Flatt plays an E-major on
the guitar, giving a lifting dissonance, a surge within the surge.

There are several periods reflected in their music. When Flatt
and Scruggs were with Mercury Records from 1948 through
1950, recording some of their early classics, the band was still
very much in the Monroe mode—banjo, fiddle, mandolin, guitar,
and bass—although the role of the banjo was of course expanded
and that of the mandolin shrunken. In fact, on their very first session in the fall of 1948, there was no mandolin: Mac Wiseman
played a second rhythm guitar and sang tenor. Clearly, Lester
and Earl wanted to distance themselves from their old boss even
at this early stage. Later, when they added dobro guitar, the mandolin would virtually disappear. Until the early 1960s, the man-

2. Lester Flatt (right) and Earl Scruggs (courtesy of Bluegrass Unlimited).

dolin was used for occasional color, with the mandolin player usually hired because of strong tenor harmony talents (Everett Lilly or longtime band member Curly Seckler, who had also worked with Charlie Monroe in his post-Bill duets).

By the time the band signed with Columbia Records, they were on their way to developing a really big sound. By 1953, they were regularly supplementing their five-piece lineup in the studio with a sixth musician, a guitarist playing closed, jazz-style "sock" chords. By autumn of 1955 they were touring with six pieces. The lineup typically included Seckler's mandolin and heroic tenor, bassist/comedian/high baritone singer Jake Tullock, hoedown fiddler/bass singer Paul Warren (who in later years would show astonishing versatility in the studio by creating fine breaks for the folk and country/western material the band was featuring) and dobro player Buck Graves, whose acoustic Hawaiian guitar stylings helped the band answer the pedal steel craze sweeping country music while keeping its sound firmly in bluegrass. In the popular comedy routines, Graves doubled as "Uncle Josh" to Tullock's "Cousin Jake."

With everyone singing (Scruggs and Graves were good baritone singers and Tullock could hit high baritone lines), the Foggy Mountain Boys could deliver powerful gospel and secular quartet harmonies and even quintets. Indeed, Jake Tullock's high baritone became a distinguishing part of the Foggy Mountain Boys sound during the latter stage of the band's career.

Years of staying together as a cohesive unit made the band tight and polished in an era when other bluegrass groups were forced to pick up and drop sidemen as economics dictated. Working microphones in a complex in-and-out stage choreography, the Foggy Mountain Boys could come through clear even on the primitive two-mike sound systems of the day. Plus this was a band in which no one laid back. From the moment the curtains parted, the Foggy Mountain Boys would awe you with their stage presence and eat you alive with their sound.

Although increasingly distancing themselves from their old boss, Flatt and Scruggs could turn out a real Monroe-style chiller with sliding minor to major third harmonies, played in insistent three-quarter time, like "No Mother in This World." But this particular 1955 recording went unissued for some 23 years; Flatt and Scruggs largely eschewed the brooding, modal "lonesome" numbers that Monroe favored and found success with sweeter sounding songs of home and love ("The Old Home Town," "Little Girl of Mine in Tennessee," "Someone Took My Place with You," "Mother Prays Loud in Her Sleep").

The Foggy Mountain Boys band rode out the crisis in country music caused by rock-n-roll, thanks not only to their huge talents (which made them a consistently popular act and earned them inclusion on the prestigious Grand Ole Opry) but also due to the regular patronage of the Martha White flour company, which sponsored the band during its road, radio, and TV appearances. Flatt and Scruggs sold tons of Martha White baking products ("With Hot Rize . . . Goodness Gracious It's Good!") and received small but consistent checks that allowed them to keep a stable band together and make consistently great music.

The Martha White sponsorship led to one of the most amusing moments in recorded bluegrass history. At their historic 1962 Carnegie Hall concert, a member of the audience called out for the Martha White theme song. Others quickly took up the cry. As the concert continued, Columbia executives began to panic, fearing their precious recording was being ruined by unremovable yells for a copyrighted commercial. But Flatt and Scruggs genially fulfilled the request to a thunderous response, Martha White Mills gladly gave permission for use of its theme, and the unplanned commercial was one of the high points of the disc.

Flatt and Scruggs came to dominate the bluegrass market, thanks to high-profile positioning during the 1960s folk boom and their playing of the theme song to TV's *The Beverly Hillbillies.* Then in 1967, producer/actor Warren Beatty used the 1949 recording of "Foggy Mountain Breakdown" in the movie *Bonnie and Clyde.* (Beatty had been turned on to bluegrass by college classmate Peter Kuykendall, who later become an active member of the Washington/Northern Virginia bluegrass scene and founded *Bluegrass Unlimited* magazine.) It was fortunate that Beatty used the original and not a re-recording, because by that time Flatt and Scruggs' music was not only shamelessly commercial, it was shamefully listless.

This drop in energy not only broke the hearts of longtime Foggy Mountain Boys fans, it caused major confusion for people just getting into bluegrass. Novices (particularly those who fancied the banjo) would be told "Whatever you do, you absolutely must listen to as much Earl Scruggs as you can" and then hear "Whatever you do, don't waste your money buying Earl Scruggs records."

The answer? Definitely buy Earl Scruggs albums, but realize that for a brief time Lester and Earl got tired of it all.

The 1960s started promisingly for Flatt and Scruggs. Manager Louise Scruggs (Earl's wife) and Columbia Records correctly saw the tremendous potential in the folk song revival, but instead of simply promoting the band's existing bluegrass as folk music (as Ralph Rinzler was to do for Bill Monroe), the group began recording a spectrum of songs by Woody Guthrie ("Hard Traveling," "Pastures of Plenty"), Donovan ("Colors"), and even Bob Dylan ("Mama You've Been on My Mind"). Earl's talented guitar-picking sons Gary and Randy became more involved in recording sessions and even shows, but their involvement further pushed the band toward folk-rock. (The Foggy Mountain Boys even played to a stoned audience at the Avalon Ballroom in San Francisco during this period, backed by the psychedelic Joshua Light Show.) Lester turned in a wry vocal on their recording of the Dylan rocker "Maggie's Farm," but "creative differences" were clearly growing between him and Scruggs. Scruggs also seemed to have nothing new to say on the banjo for the time being, and in 1969 the Flatt and Scruggs partnership ended. Their final public appearance together is believed to have been riding on the Tennessee float in Richard M. Nixon's inaugural parade. (The following year, Earl was back in Washington, D.C., only this time appearing with his sons at a major anti-Vietnam war rally!)

In this musical divorce Lester ended up with most of the "children," using the former Foggy Mountain Boys to found the bluegrass-oriented Nashville Grass. Earl joined with his sons and other young musicians to form the folk-rock-oriented Earl Scruggs Revue. Those new to bluegrass are urged to approach the late-1960s period of the Foggy Mountain Boys with caution.

There was a lot of stuff that just didn't gel. Their final serious bluegrass-style recordings for Columbia would have to be the sessions that resulted in *The Fabulous Sound of Flatt and Scruggs* and to a lesser extent their collaboration with flatpicking guitar whiz Doc Watson, *Strictly Instrumental*. (These albums are out of print but the material should soon be included in CD collections of their final recording sessions.)

For mainstream bluegrassers, recordings by the Nashville Grass are bound to be the most satisfying of the post–Flatt and Scruggs era. Lester particularly got back in stride when he signed with RCA and started turning out solid country-flavored bluegrass. His novelty songs from this period are especially fun, with "I Can't Tell the Boys from the Girls" and "Backing to Birmingham" becoming instant classics when given Flatt's droll delivery.

The Nashville Grass was also one very hot band. Even as ill health began to plague Flatt (after major heart-bypass surgery he kept touring by adding a registered nurse to his retinue), he lost little of his singing abilities and none of his fluid rhythm guitar style. Among standout sidemen in the band during Flatt's final years were Foggy Mountain Boys veteran fiddler Paul Warren, ace banjoists Vic Jordan and Kenny Ingram, mandolin/vocalist wunderkind Marty Stuart (now, of course, a hugely successful country music star), plus Curly Seckler, a mainstay of the late 1950s Foggy Mountain Boys and probably one of bluegrass music's greatest tenor harmony singers.

Over on the other side of the Flatt/Scruggs schism, the Earl Scruggs Revue had much more going for it than embittered Foggy Mountain Boys fans and hostile critics might have you believe. Earl seemed to regain strength and enthusiasm playing with his sons. He was the subject of an appreciative documentary, *Earl Scruggs: His Family and Friends*, which featured guest appearances by Joan Baez, Bob Dylan, Wiley and Zeke Morris (with whom Earl had worked as a young man and who popularized a song that later became a big Flatt and Scruggs hit, "The Salty Dog Blues"), plus Bill Monroe, who had reconciled individually with Lester and Earl. Scruggs was clearly happy and his music showed greater flow. Add to that the real talents of the Scruggs sons and the Revue was at times a pretty good group.

You might find a used Scruggs Revue record worth picking up if the price is right.

Flatt died in 1979. Scruggs visited him during his last days and the former partners parted after something of a reconciliation. But the careers of these great musicians should not be judged by their final few years together.

Lester Flatt, Earl Scruggs, and the Foggy Mountain Boys were a true phenomenon. And the highest praise may be that even though they had one of the most venerated bands in bluegrass history, it is perhaps the one that has been the least successfully imitated.

Lester Flatt, Earl Scruggs, and the Foggy Mountain Boys. *1948–1959,* **Bear Family 15472 (complete Mercury and early Columbia sessions)**

————. *1959–1963,* **Bear Family 15559 (further Columbia material, including the complete 1962 Carnegie Hall concert)**

————. *The Complete Mercury Sessions,* **Mercury 512644**

————. *Blue Ridge Cabin Home,* **Rounder 102 (early Columbia material, mostly pre-dobro)**

————. *The Golden Era,* **Rounder SS05 (middle Columbia period with the six-piece Foggy Mountain Boys band)**

————. *Don't Get Above Your Raisin',* **Rounder SS08 (more classic Columbia sessions and six-piece Foggy Mountain Boys band)**

————. *Folk Songs of Our Land,* **Columbia 8630 (folk music)**

————. *Hard Travelin',* **Columbia 8751 (features "Ballad of Jed Clampett" plus several Woody Guthrie songs)**

————. *The Fabulous Sound of Flatt and Scruggs,* **Columbia 9055 (contains several Carter Family numbers; audible mandolin)**

————. *Final Fling (One Last Time),* **Columbia 9945**

————, **with Doc Watson.** *Strictly Instrumental,* **Columbia 9443**

Lester Flatt and the Nashville Grass. *Lester Raymond Flatt,* **Flying Fish 015**

———. *Greatest Bluegrass Hits,* CMH 4503

Earl Scruggs. *Nashville's Rock,* Columbia 1007

———. *Earl Scruggs: His Family and Friends,* Columbia 30584 (documentary soundtrack featuring Bob Dylan and the Byrds)

Marty Stuart. *Once upon a Time,* CMH 8000 (a collection of tracks by the Nashville Grass featuring Stuart)

FOUR

WHITE DOVE WILL MOURN IN SORROW
The Stanley Brothers

One day a salesman for RCA walked into a record store in
Harlan, Kentucky with his supervisor. The salesman asked
who the biggest selling artist was, thinking the answer would
be Eddy Arnold. When the dealer said it was the Stanley
Brothers, the supervisor rared back like a judge and said, 'Who
are the Stanley Brothers?' The reply was that they were the
hottest thing in the country.
—Carl Sauceman (quoted in Gary B. Reid's notes to
The Stanley Brothers and the Clinch Mountain Boys,
1949–1952, Bear Family Records BCD 15564)

Often the terms "bluegrass" and "mountain music" are used in-
terchangeably and rather incorrectly. In the case of the Stanley
sound, there is a close and true connection.

Ralph and Carter Stanley and the Clinch Mountain Boys
steeped their music in the modal tradition brought to the Appalachians by settlers from the British Isles, much as Bill Monroe
had reveled in the African-American blues. What has become

41

known as "the Stanley sound" is powerful, recognizable, and unique. Indeed, many bluegrass connoisseurs rank the Stanleys along with Monroe and Flatt and Scruggs as the great triumvirate of bluegrass.

For a time, the Stanley Brothers and the Clinch Mountain Boys were virtual clones of Bill Monroe and His Blue Grass Boys. Their recording of Monroe's "Molly and Tenbrooks" was released in September 1948, long before Monroe had recorded his own version of this now-famous "bluegrass race horse song": The Stanleys learned it from Monroe's concerts and radio shows. They recorded this and other Monroe material at the urging of their mandolin player, Darrell "Pee Wee" Lambert, who had become a near Monroe fanatic. As had occurred with Flatt and Scruggs, Bill Monroe himself had no way of knowing that he started a musical genre whose performers would one day honor him as its father. No one did. So at the time, Monroe concluded he was being robbed of his creative output and was furious. He left Columbia Records for Decca soon after Columbia had signed the Stanleys, and many bluegrass historians believe the events were linked. A few years later, in 1951, there was a reconciliation when Ralph took a break from music and Carter joined Monroe's band.

The Stanleys moved quickly from imitation to innovation. Drawing on their mountain roots, they achieved a synthesis of Anglo-American modalities, old-time string band music, and Monroe-style bluegrass that has never been rivaled. Ironically, Ralph's initially unseasoned banjo playing helped in this regard. Before he had smoothed out his three-finger picking technique, Ralph relied heavily on a two-finger approach similar to the old "double thumbing" style. He remains a fine practitioner of the old-time "frailing" style of banjo playing, in which a combination of thumb picking and downward fingernail brushing is used to sound the strings. (The style is also called "clawhammer" from the position the picking hand takes.) Just as Monroe was inspired by his mother's fiddle and accordion playing, Lucy Smith Stanley's sons were thrilled by her fine banjo frailing.

British songs with somber themes sung in minor keys, which survived in America as mountain ballads, became hallmarks of the Stanley sound. "Man of Constant Sorrow" and the murder ballad "Pretty Polly," both of which were sung a cappella by Fitzhugh Stanley during his sons' childhood, entered the Clinch Mountain Boys repertoire and remain tours-de-force for Ralph.

The influence of the elder Stanleys on their sons went much further than providing musical technique or material. Ralph and Carter developed a sense of home that suffused their music in many ways. There was the general warm nostalgia for a familiar, safe and simpler place that, as we've seen, was common to the country music enjoyed by southerners who had trekked to big cities searching for jobs or whose lives were being impacted by modernization.

But for Ralph and Carter—spending days, weeks, and even months on the road and being featured at major radio stations throughout the South—every comforting thought of home was infected with terrible dread. What if home was lost forever? The brothers often discussed what the world would be like when their parents were no longer alive. What if they came back home and didn't know anybody? What if the years caused their closeknit mountain community to vanish? As modern society becomes so faceless that we rarely know our own neighbors ("Gee, I thought that guy at your back door lived with you. I didn't know he was breaking in. . . ."), the anxieties powerfully expressed in such Stanley classics as "Rank Strangers," "The Fields Have Turned Brown," and "White Dove" no longer seem quaint.

Much has been written about the Stanleys' career and a detailed biography of the band will not be attempted here, except to say that each period of the Clinch Mountain Boys' history offers something of interest: the Rich-R-Tone sessions that sounded most like the pre-bluegrass string bands; the Monroesque Columbia recordings (which also yielded some of the band's finest gospel quartets); and the years with Mercury and Starday when the brothers' sound really came together with such great sidemen as bassist/vocalist George Shuffler and fiddlers Leslie Keith (who popularized "Black Mountain Blues," also known as "Black Mountain Rag"), Chubby Anthony, Ralph Mayo, Benny Martin, and others.

Even the later sessions done for the King record company are interesting. At the first was committed to wax the still widely requested vocal "How Mountain Girls Can Love" and the banjo instrumental "Clinch Mountain Backstep." During this period, the Stanleys emphasized a second guitar as a lead instrument. Perhaps this was intended to make the band sound more "folky" during the 1960s, but in recent years Ralph has generally retained the second guitar in preference to a mandolin in his band, so its presence has become part of the Stanley sound. Also during the '60s the Stanleys recorded a lot, including a wealth of in-concert material. That has delighted their fans, although it has led some wags to dub them the most over-recorded band in bluegrass history.

Carter's incredible contributions as a lead singer came not only from the quality of his voice but from the depth of emotion he loaned to each song. The man was almost a mountain Hank Williams. The early recordings of the Clinch Mountain Boys in particular feature trios with an almost perfect polish, burnished at the end of the lines by Ralph's mountain-sounding, mountain-high harmonies.

Unfortunately, like Hank Williams and so many other poets and musicians, Carter's life was shortened by ill health worsened by years of drinking. Ironically, the song that brought the Stanleys to the attention of the Rich-R-Tone record company in 1947 was "Little Glass of Wine." Later, Carter would sing powerfully on "Whiskey and Jail" and other songs detailing the miseries of drink.

After Carter's death in 1966, Ralph considered quitting music altogether rather than continuing along the miles and through the years without his beloved brother. (He has often said that if he were not a musician he would want to be a veterinarian. In all likelihood, it was at this time that all creatures great and small around Dickenson County nearly gained a kindly new friend.)

But there was an outpouring of support from legions of Stanley Brothers fans, so Ralph persevered. In selecting new singing partners who sounded like Carter, he was aided by the fact that most of them—notably Larry Sparks, Roy Lee Centers, and Keith Whitley—not only grew up loving the Stanley sound but even came from within a few counties of Ralph's corner of Virginia, so their vocalizations about lonesome pines, midnight rivers, and the hills of home were no mere intellectualizations.

3. Ralph and Carter Stanley (courtesy of Bluegrass Unlimited).

It is sad to note that Ralph Stanley has indeed been a man of constant sorrows where guitarist/lead singers have been concerned: a long-running local feud culminated in the beating and shooting death of Roy Lee Centers in 1974, and Keith Whitley died of an alcohol overdose in 199? just as he was achieving major success in Nashville as one of the stars of the new country music.

Ralph Stanley has for some reason never received credit for his impressive ability to keep adapting great material to his ultra-traditionalist bluegrass style. His beautiful arrangement of Jesse Winchester's Vietnam-era lament "Brand New Tennessee Waltz" and the broodingly poignant portrait of a May/September love affair in "Room at the Top of the Stairs" are just two examples. Most recent Stanley albums contain such songs.

The fans of "the Stanley sound" are many and they are fiercely loyal. And with reason.

The Stanley Brothers and the Clinch Mountain Boys. *1949–1952,* **Bear Family 15564 (Columbia sessions)**

————. *1953–1959,* **Bear Family 15681 (Mercury and Blue Ridge sessions)**

————. *Early Stanley Brothers,* **King 7000 (King and Starday material)**

————. *The Stanley Brothers,* **Copper Creek 5501 through 5512 (live and studio recordings from 1955 to 1962)**

————. *The Stanley Brothers Together for the Last Time,* **Rebel 1512**

————. *Little Old Country Church House,* **County 738 (first in a four-volume County collection of major Stanley recordings)**

————. *Long Journey Home,* **County 739**

————. *Uncloudy Day,* **County 753**

————. *The Stanley Brothers of Virginia,* **County 754**

Ralph Stanley. *Classic Bluegrass,* **Rebel 1109 (with Roy Lee Centers)**

————. *A Man and His Music,* **Rebel 1530**

————. *Saturday Night and Sunday Morning,* **Freeland 9001**

Crime and Punishment, Bluegrass Style

Any culture is a study in contrasts. The heights of a Golden Era often overlook the depths of a Dark Age. Classical arts have lived contemporaneous with barbaric savagery. From time immemorial, flowering societies have had a stinking underside of war, torture, and forced labor.

Southern mountain and rural cultures were neither wholly good nor wholly evil. But between the idyllic joys celebrated in "My Old Kentucky Home" and the degenerate brutality depicted in Deliverance is a middle ground where love and faith lived side by side with violent passions. Notable songs of crime and tragedy—some inspired by real events—have found their way into the bluegrass repertoire.

Some of these crimes literally crossed an ocean. Several bluegrass standards derive directly from old ballads that arrived in America with settlers from the British Isles. For example, "The Knoxville Girl" refers to "a town we all know well," but this Knoxville was originally in England, not Tennessee. A popular duet in the early days of country music (see the section on "Bluegrass Brothers" in Appendix One), it is also a graphically violent tale of a suitor who inexplicably turns on his intended. Sneering that she will never be his bride, the killer is incited to greater violence as she pleads for her life ("I only beat her more/ Until the ground around her all with her blood did flow . . .").

Although I've yet to hear any singers who seem to glory in this horrific crime, the fact that "The Knoxville Girl" features about the sweetest melody and harmony of any traditional ballad makes listening to it a particularly unsettling experience.

A haunting use of a relative minor chord gives more appropriate notes of tragedy to "Down in the Willow Garden," another oft-recorded bluegrass murder ballad with English origins. Again sung from the perspective of the killer, the tale is told of the murder of Rose Connelly (apparently for her money, an idea put into her suitor's head by his father). Rose's death is Shakespearean in its drama: She is first poisoned, then stabbed, then thrown in the river for extra measure. The killer ends up on the scaffold awaiting death and eternal damnation ("My race is run beneath the sun/ The devil is waiting for me . . .") while his father looks on.

The final drowning of Rose Connelly reminds us that riverbanks are fraught with danger for women in bluegrass ballads. A famous murder is committed on the "Banks of the Ohio" by a jilted suitor who is captured by the sheriff and returned to the scene of the crime ("He said, Young man/ Come now let's go/ To the banks of the Ohio").

The deep woods is the setting for the death of "Pretty Polly," and a modal scale immediately sets a menacing atmosphere for this tale of premeditated murder. A fellow named Willy kills his girlfriend, apparently because she has become pregnant (in some versions she sings of "the way you have led my poor body astray"). Lured away on the pretense of another tryst, she is led to "a newly dug grave with a spade lying by." In some versions, Willy rides off after his crime "leaving nothing behind but the wild birds to mourn." But in a more satisfying and psychologically fascinating version, he becomes deranged, riding straight to the sheriff and announcing, "I've killed Pretty Polly/ I'm trying to get away."

The killer of "Poor Ellen Smith" ("How she was found!") is quickly tracked down after her shooting and definitely suffers. Sentenced to prison, he is haunted by her image ("At night I see Ellen through my bitter tears").

That may be scant comfort for those who are understandably nauseated by all this violence against women. There is some small comfort in songs in which the female is the criminal. One of the most successful villainesses in bluegrass is "The Girl in the Blue Velvet Band." A young man strolling in San Francisco one evening is flirted with by a seductively beautiful woman (". . . with eyes that seemed to expand/ And hair so rich and so brilliant/ Entwined in a blue velvet band"). Unbeknownst to the smitten fellow, the lady is one step ahead of the law. She slips a stolen $10,000 diamond into his pocket and leaves just before the police sweep around the corner and arrest him. He ends up in San Quentin, where in a midnight moment of horrible clairvoyance, he realizes that the girl is dying. He does his time and leaves prison, understandably dismayed by the whole experience.

"Doin' My Time" is the title of another bluegrass classic, only this one focuses on the punishment ("On this old rock pile/ With a ball and chain/ They call me by a number not a name . . ."). The prisoner vows to settle down and quit his rowdy ways once he's released. True love will seemingly reward these good intentions ("She'll be waitin' for me/ When I've done my time").

Just as settlers from the British Isles brought their favorite ballads with them, some unfortunately brought a propensity for violent grudges. The Scots-Irish names of Hatfield and McCoy remind us that many hillbilly feuds echoed the clan warfare of the old country. One of the most moving songs of family conflict is "The Hills of Roan County," in which the singer is forced to kill one of his fiancée's kinsmen ("Her brother stabbed me for some unknown reason/ Just three months later I'd taken Tom's life"). He is tried, quickly convicted of murder ("Not a man in that county would speak one kind word"), sentenced to life at hard labor, and finally seen off by his mother and sister ("And the last words I heard were Willy, God bless you/ Were Willy, God bless you, God bless you, goodbye!"). He ends by asking his fellow prisoners to help him communicate with the outside world ("Place one of my songs in your letters for me").

One can only wish the sociopath who killed the "Knoxville Girl" had been tried in "The Hills of Roan County."

Sometimes, death comes before dishonor—or at least before the revelation of dishonor. The protagonist of "The Long Black Veil" (written by Mary John Wilkin and Danny Dill) recounts how he was mistakenly identified as the killer in a stabbing but refused to offer his alibi—he had been committing adultery at the time with his best friend's wife. The singer, now a ghost, ends by telling how his lover stoically watched his hanging but, ten years later, still mourns over his grave while wearing a long black veil.

Talk about taking responsibility for your actions!

FIVE

NOT A SECOND FIDDLE

Don Reno and Red Smiley

When you'd play towns, you'd have bankers and lawyers, even
back then—some were ashamed to admit they liked it. . . .
—Don Reno to interviewer Bill Vernon on the early
audiences for banjo playing

Admirers of nimble-fingered banjoist Don Reno are fond of
claiming that had war not intervened, we would probably today
be calling bluegrass banjo technique not "Scruggs picking" but
"Reno picking."

Reno was another brilliant and advanced product of the North
Carolina school of three-finger picking for the 5-string banjo,
which had arisen as an alternative to the thumb-pick/fingernail-
brush "frailing" and thumb/single finger "double thumbing"
approaches that then dominated rural music. (See the section on
banjo players in Chapter 15 for more on the North Carolina pickers.) In the early 1940s, the Bluegrass Boys played at radio station
WSPA in Spartanburg, South Carolina. There, Bill Monroe met
and later jammed with Reno.

Monroe had only had his band together a few years and was

51

still developing his style of ensemble music. Not only was Reno
exciting on the fast-paced breakdowns, he could also adapt his
playing to the bluesy vocals, including waltzes, which Monroe
loved. Monroe was apparently as excited about adding the banjo
to his band as Glenn Miller was when he hit on the idea of using
the clarinet to carry the lead lines usually handled by the trumpet in big bands. Both had found "the sound."

Reno had a job if he wanted it. But World War II was being
fought and he had enlisted. He passed the physical and went off
to the Pacific theater. Dave "Stringbean" Akeman later played
the 5-string with the Blue Grass Boys, but as we have seen it was
another excellent North Carolinian picker—Earl Scruggs—who
brought the instrument into its own. (Scruggs, who had received

4. Don Reno and Red Smiley with Bill Harrell (center) (photo by Tom Henderson).

a legitimate exemption because he was supporting his widowed mother, did not serve in the war.)

Reno did join the Blue Grass Boys after the war ended and Scruggs had departed. Unfortunately he did not stay long enough to participate in Monroe's next foray into the studio. This important session (which featured vocalist Mac Wiseman) had been delayed because of a nationwide interruption of recording during a royalties dispute between record companies and songwriters.

If Reno was disappointed at having missed major opportunities for exposure, it didn't hold him back. He spent time working with Arthur Smith, composer of the hit "Guitar Boogie" and a catchy answer-back instrumental called "Feudin' Banjos"—later to become a national smash when used in the 1971 movie *Deliverance* (and subsequently the subject of a major lawsuit because it had been assumed that "Feudin' Banjos," also known by then as "Mockin' Banjos" and "Duelin' Banjos," was a traditional public domain folk tune).

Later, at a radio station in Roanoke, Reno met Red Smiley, a fellow North Carolinian who was an excellent singer and rhythm guitarist. They clicked and joined forces.

The group effortlessly straddled bluegrass and what was generically known in the late 1950s and early 1960s as "country music." Most of the greatest Reno and Smiley compositions were released on King, notably the gospel number "I'm Using My Bible for a Road Map" (with its running metaphor of life as a difficult journey over rough roads and around detours, owing more than a little to the musicians' existence on tour); the hot banjo instrumental "Dixie Breakdown"; and that classic of unrequited love, "I Know You're Married But I Love You Still."

They were ably backed by solid sidemen, including fiddler Mack Magaha and Ronnie Reno, Don's son and one of the most underrated bluegrass mandolinists of all time. (Recently Ronnie has joined with siblings Dale and Don Wayne in a successful country 'grass act called, of course, the Reno Brothers.)

Reno and Smiley temporarily separated and performed separately, with Don having a particularly fruitful collaboration with singer/guitarist Bill Harrell. They reunited prior to Smiley's death in 1972.

The similarities and differences between Reno and Smiley and Flatt and Scruggs are interesting. Both partnerships featured a hot banjo player set off by a genial song stylist. Red Smiley was one of the finest bluegrass vocalists of all time. He will appeal to many first-time listeners because he does not have the stereotypical raw, nasal, cut-through-the-banjo-pickin' bluegrass voice.

Reno—partly because of his talents as a guitarist and partly to differentiate himself from Scruggs—developed a colorful, intricate banjo style in parallel with his straight-ahead bluegrass picking. His use of chord progressions to express melody lines, often sounded with strumming more than picking patterns, owes much to jazz guitar. His rapid single-note arpeggios foreshadowed the melodic and chromatic newgrass banjo styles that were to follow him (and whose young exponents usually venerated Reno as a banjo pioneer). Indeed, some banjo players have speculated that if Reno's influence has not been as great as his extremely high reputation it's only because his total style is downright difficult to master.

Who was greater, Reno (who died in 1984) or Earl Scruggs? Both were so good the question not only becomes impossible to answer but irrelevant. Both—with the lead-singing partners they fortunately didn't overshadow—should be heard forever.

Don Reno and Bill Harrell. *Bluegrass Favorites,* **Rural Rhythm 171**

————. *Bluegrass on My Mind,* **Starday 481–498**

Don Reno, Red Smiley, and the Tennessee Cutups. *20 Bluegrass Originals,* **Deluxe 7906**

————. *The Early Reno and Smiley,* **King 7001**

————. *A Day in the Country,* **CCLP 0106 (live performance)**

————. *Songs from Yesterday,* **Rebel 1661 (reissue of classic Wango Records material)**

————. *Last Time Together,* **Starday 465–498**

Red Smiley and the Bluegrass Cutups. *Bluegrass Favorites,* **Rural Rhythm 160**

SIX

SOME KIND OF
AN ANSWER
Jimmy Martin

Music should strike fire in the heart of man, and bring tears
from the eyes of woman.

—Beethoven

It was one of the most reprehensible practical jokes I ever pulled,
and one day I will pay dearly for it.

I was at a major bluegrass festival with a friend when I saw
that Jimmy Martin was scheduled to perform at the main stage
area that afternoon.

"Jimmy Martin is a very fine performer," I told my friend. "But
he has a very low-key folky style. He's very laid back and does-
n't project well. He could use a course in ego strengthening.
We'd better get there early and make sure we get a seat up *real*
close. Up close is the best place to appreciate Jimmy Martin."

Well, at least the very first and the very last statements were true.
Martin *is* a very fine performer, and up close *is* the best place to appreciate him. (And I guess if I were a die-hard heavy metal rock
fan, I'd be the kind of person to sit right in front of the speakers.)

55

I took my trusting friend and guided her to some seats at second row center. We were soon joined by Pete and Eddie, two buddies of mine who are born-again Jimmy Martin fans. My friend should have known something was up when Eddie leaned over to her and grinned.

"Remember," he said. "Jimmy loves you."

Anyone who knows the irrepressible Jimmy Martin and his music will have an all-too-clear picture of what happened next. Martin was scarcely introduced when he bounced to the front of the stage (nearly running over the MC), resplendent (as usual) in shiny dark red sports coat, checkerboard (no kidding) cowboy hat, black slacks, and white shoes. He yelped out "Hi y'all!" nearly popping the cones out of the PA system, and as the Sunny Mountain Boys band joined ranks alongside him, hit the big wide guitar strum.

The band crashed into "Freeborn Man." Pete, Eddie, and I cheered, whistled, and stomped. My friend, as I well knew, blushes easily when she's made the center of attention. She turned pink. Martin looked at the four of us out of the corner of his eye. That eye developed a more-than-usual gleam.

The audience tapped their feet, applauded the hard-as-nails banjo picking that is a trademark of Martin's bands, and looked with amusement at Martin's rowdy little second row fan club.

My friend laughed nervously. She turned rose-colored. She looked for an escape route. There was none; she was surrounded by three completely effusive idiots. We applauded Jimmy's every inflection. We screamed at every guitar run he snapped into the microphone.

"The King of Bluegrass!" I yelled. "The King of Bluegrass!"

Martin's grin got wider, his manner even cockier. Pete, Eddie, and I got even more exuberant. My friend got crimson and sank into her seat. From below me I heard a voice say simply and sweetly, "I'll get you for this."

I believe she will. I still fully expect a nasty measure of embarrassment, good-natured or otherwise, to be my fate.

Martin, a Tennessean, came to fame as a Blue Grass Boy. He was lead singer on some of Bill Monroe's most impassioned autobiographical "true song" duets of the early 1950s (such as

"Memories of Mother and Dad" and "Letter from My Darlin'").
Later he went out on his own, in a brief collaboration with the
Osborne Brothers, then eventually heading up Jimmy Martin
and the Sunny Mountain Boys.

Martin's band reached critical mass with a lineup including
tenor Paul Williams on mandolin (not to be confused with the
pop music composer) and baritone J. D. Crowe on banjo. If Flatt
and Scruggs gave Bill Monroe the classic combination that finally
defined bluegrass, Martin found his own musical destiny with
Williams and Crowe. Williams could write and sing to match
Martin's intensity. And Crowe had a style that can only be described as a hi-tech machine gun firing musical lasers and then
bending the beams every once in a while for added effect.

Today, every young banjo picker signing on for a stint as a
Sunny Mountain Boy is expected to have the Crowe style down
cold (or perhaps I should say down hot). Great banjoists who followed Crowe and went on to make their own marks in bluegrass
have included Vic Jordan, Bill Emerson, and Alan Munde. Martin also favors bright and sturdy mandolin picking, and he found
an exceptional early replacement for Williams in the person of
Vernon Derrick.

Although Martin, like many other bluegrass greats, has recently had a revolving door of sidemen and relied heavily on his
classic repertoire in concert, he has maintained high standards in
his band. For one thing, live performances are supposed to
sound just like the record. When the band cracks into "Sunny
Side of the Mountain" (a lyrical Carter Family number that Martin has turned into a hard-driving signature song), you know
you'll be pinned to your seat and the crowd will be howling.
Even today, it's a pleasure and an education to watch Martin—
the veteran and taskmaster—backstage instructing a new sideman in the harmony lines or instrumental accents that he expects
and demands as part of the Sunny Mountain Boys sound.

Martin's brilliant vocalizings have earned him a reputation as
one of the greatest bluegrass lead singers ever to step up to a microphone. He's been hugely successful at converting country-
and-western chart climbers into bluegrass classics, songs such as
the old Gene Autry lament "20/20 Vision" and in particular

"Milwaukee Here I Come," a hit for country music deity George Jones that Martin has made his own—no mean feat. Martin's brash delivery has also been excellently suited for a series of no-velty-type songs: "Save It! Save It!" (recorded with the Osbornes, replete with wolf whistles and risque lyrics), "Guitar Pickin' President," "I Go Ape," and "I Wish I Was Sixteen Again (and Knew What I Know Now)."

Despite successful guest appearances on the Grand Ole Opry and a home base now in the Nashville area, Jimmy Martin has never fulfilled his dream of becoming an Opry regular. This lack of an invitation to join that select roster may have something to do with the fact that Martin's personality is, well, rather strong. As he likes to say, "My daddy always said if a man asks you a question, always give him some kind of an answer."

But Martin had a true career highlight in 1972 when he was chosen by the Nitty Gritty Dirt Band to represent hard-driving bluegrass on their landmark collaboration with traditional-style country musicians, *Will the Circle Be Unbroken* album. Mar-tin rose to the occasion mightily, reprising his greatest hits and proving to be a solid rock for what had been an artistically risky project.

Whether it's at stageside or in front of your stereo speakers, enjoy the checkered demon from Sneedville, Tennessee. And sit up close.

Jimmy Martin and the Sunny Mountain Boys. *You Don't Know My Mind,* **Rounder SS 21 (1956–1966 Decca/MCA, cuts featuring J. D. Crowe and Paul Williams)**
———. *20 Greatest Hits,* **DL 7863**
———. *Greatest Hits,* **HT 213**

Humor in Bluegrass: A Baggy Pants Dozen

Bill Monroe's senatorial stage demeanor has given bluegrass a bad rap as be-ing humorless (indeed, some Monroe devotees seem like they'd rather hit a sour note than smile on stage). Although Monroe has been variously (and ac-curately) described as "a man of princely bearing and precious few words" and "like a statue walking," he's actually possessed of a wry sense of humor and has featured comedy in his act.

Bill's early bands, after he broke up with brother Charlie, had a good-time feel to them. The Kentuckians (the never-recorded precursor to the Blue Grass Boys) featured a jug player. Monroe's early recordings with his band on RCA sound at times like a happy mountain string band with comments and asides, reaching a high point with Monroe's astounding 1939 recording of "Dog House Blues" (Muleskinner Blues, RCA-2494-2-R). This tale of a husband forced by a disgruntled wife to sleep with the family pooch comes with barks and baying, courtesy of the Blue Grass Boys themselves.

Wacky comedians and zany skits have long been part of the music, but some of the best moments have regrettably not been preserved because they came in the form of stage routines: Don Reno and Red Smiley's "Chicken Hot Rod" act (performed largely in drag), the rapidly escalating war of mandolinist John Duffey vs. banjoist Eddie Adcock during the classic Country Gentlemen version of "Duelin' Banjos," and the vaudeville-style two-man comedy interludes of Foggy Mountain Boys veterans "Cousin Jake" Tullock and "Uncle Josh" Graves:

"I dreamed last night I won a million dollars in Las Vegas."

"I dreamed last night I was with a beautiful blond and a beautiful redhead."

"Why didn't you call me up to share one with me?"

"I tried, but you was in Las Vegas!"

In more recent times, Hot Rize had its takeoff on country-and-western music, Red Knuckles and the Trailblazers.

Many of the early bluegrass comedy routines were heavily influenced by the baggy pants humor of the old touring country music tent shows (which in turn owed a debt to the traveling medicine show). But Mitch Jayne, bassist and MC of the Dillards, developed a droll front-man style that was part storytelling, part standup comedy. Jayne not only used his humor to entertain audiences but to cue audiences in on what his friends were doing (a gag about mandolinist Dean Webb's small hands led audiences to watch his hands when he played solos). Jayne retired from music and is now writing and making his mark in the folk storytelling revival (Stories from Home, Volumes 1 and 2, Wildstone Audio).

Below are some mirth points of bluegrass music. (Not listed here from the Nashville/country-and-western side of things—but highly recommended—are the novelty songs of Grandpa Jones and just about anything by the duo of Homer and Jethro.)

"The Coupon Song," Bill Monroe and His Blue Grass Boys. Muleskinner Blues, RCA 2494. Bassist Bill "Cousin Wilbur" Wesbrooks sings that he saved enough coupons to get himself a wife—now he's saving up for a divorce. This same period gave us "Dog House Blues," in which the band offered jugbandish humor.

"Still Trying to Get to Little Rock," the Stanley Brothers. Folk Song Festival, King 12-791. This classic routine, based on the old "Arkansas Traveler" stories, was recorded by the Stanleys several times with many verses and variations. For instance, a stranger asks a farmer for directions and gets hilariously unhelpful answers:

"Hello there, farmer."

"Why, hello there, stranger."

"Can I cross this creek?"

"I don't see why not. A whole flock of ducks crossed less'n an hour ago."

"But is the water deep?"

"It only come up to here on the ducks."

I like to think there's a Zen-like quality to all this and that the Traveler is actually the equivalent of the Novice Monk on a spiritual quest (Enlightenment = Little Rock). The Farmer is a Master, seemingly confounding the search but actually giving wise guidance. The exchanges are therefore the bluegrass equivalent of the Zen Buddhist spiritual riddles known as "koans."

I certainly hope no one takes this theory seriously.

Comedy Songs of Lulu Belle and Scotty, Lulu Belle and Scotty Wiseman, Mar-Lu 8903. Scotty Wiseman composed such serious country classics as "You Go To Your Church and I'll Go To Mine" and "Have I Told You Lately That I Love You?") and in 1936 Lulu Belle actually outpolled Kate Smith as "National Radio Queen." But as "The Hayloft Sweethearts" they were also a major comedy act, as this tape reflects. How can you possibly resist such titles as "Shut the Door, They're Coming Through the Window," "When Grandpa Got His Whiskers Caught in the Zipper of His Shirt," or "Store-Bought Teeth"?

"No Curb Service Anymore," The Lonesome Pine Fiddlers. Windy Mountain, Bear Family ECD 501. The increasingly suburbanized world of the 1950s South becomes the scene of flirtation and heartbreak, as a lovely ingenue blinks and winks her way to a good time and free meals from a smitten drive-in restaurant attendant.

"Guitar Pickin' President," Jimmy Martin and the Sunny Mountain Boys. You Don't Know My Mind, Rounder SS 21. Every four years, before the first Tuesday in November, I sing this song to myself and think, "Why not?" Piano-tinkling (Truman) and sax-blowing (Clinton) presidents are okay, I guess, but they're not the real thing. This track is also a real Cold War classic, with its references to appeasing Khrushchev by letting him bring his balalaika along.

"Mama Blues," Flatt and Scruggs at Carnegie Hall, Columbia CS8845; also on reissue Flatt and Scruggs, 1959–1963, Bear Family 15559. "Making the banjo talk" is no longer a mere figure of speech when Earl Scruggs, who used special tuning pegs to effect on the tour-de-force instrumentals "Flint Hill Special" and "Randy Lynn Rag," uses them to create a dialogue between a harried parent and a demanding child. Must be heard to be believed.

"The Biggest Whatever," the Dillards. Wheatstraw Suite, Elektra 74035. Rodney Dillard and a friend were out walking in the Ozark Mountains one day when they saw what other reputable eyewitnesses have reported in mountain wilderness areas from America to the Himalayas: a large unknown bipedal primate, popularly known as a Sasquatch or Yeti. (No, it wasn't a bear.) Like other eyewitnesses they were left terrified but unharmed. The friend grew up to produce the movie Harry and the Hendersons, about a family that adopts a friendly Bigfoot. Rodney grew up to write this.

"If You Like Bluegrass," The Extended Playboys. The Extended Playboys. This is a real collector's item, featuring Country Cooking members Peter Wernick, Tony Trischka, John Miller, and others. The band's name refers not to any physical attributes (as far as I know) but to the medium of an extended-play 45 rpm record. This particular track contains about every bluegrass instrumental cliché known, with Jimmy Martin–style accents and reverb. Also on the record: the world's fastest version of "Foggy Mountain Breakdown," accomplished by dropping a measure of music before every chord change, allowing the pickers to reach the "fine" line in record time.

Y'All Come: Bluegrass Humor, Jim and Jesse McReynolds. Epic LN-24144. There'll be grins aplenty as the boys sing about the joys of banjos, biscuits, and unexpected guests.

"Tired Iron," Pumpkin Ridge Meet the Punks. Tired Iron Auto Wrecking [Cassette, no number]. This Portland, Oregon, group offers this track as an affectionate send-up of the various home goods and patent medicine companies that have sponsored bluegrass on the radio: "Goodness gracious what a junkyard—Tired Iron!"

"Yellow Submarine," Charles River Valley Boys. Beatle Country, Elektra 74006. High-spirited hillbilly hijinx aboard the famous Lennon/McCartney undersea boat. Scored for old-time banjo, bluegrass trio, wind-up music toy, gunshots, and gurgles.

The Walls We Bounce Off Of, John Hartford. Small Dog a-Barkin 394. No listing of the offbeat would be in step without Hartford, a true American original. A sample of titles from this recent outing: "Fourteen Pole Cats on a Chevy Camaro," "The All Collision All Explosion Song," and "Hooter Thunkit."

Into the Twangy-First Century, Run C&W. MCA 10727. These boys get the "baker's dozen" position, and they deserve it. The premise of this album is that the Burns family (Dad Burns, Au Burns, Side Burns, et al) moved from Harlan County, Kentucky, to Detroit as part of the mass migration of country folk finding work in northern factories. Once in Motor City, the Burns clan discovered the "Motown" sound of pop rhythm-n-blues and decided "to play it as God intended it—bluegrass style." Thus you get Stevie Wonder, James Brown, and Holland-Dozier-Holland classics played with an upbeat on this offbeat CD.

When this production first came out I gave it a highly unenthusiastic review on the grounds that Run C&W's approach (stereotyped nasal vocals, barnyard imitations, and unrelenting washboard playing) was pretty heavy-handed and thus unhumorous. A sackful of angry letters (well, at least three) to Bluegrass Unlimited magazine, lots of airplay, and solid sales show that listener opinion was by no means on my side. Meanwhile, the boys have decided neither to sink nor swim with their second release, Row vs. Wade, MCA 11041. Listen for yourself. Maybe you'll 'preciate it.

(Dis?)Honorable mention: P.D.Q. Bach—Black Forest Blue Grass, Peter Schickele. Vanguard 79427. Julliard-trained composer Schickele has made a successful second career spoofing classical music styles and scholarship with his "discoveries" of hitherto unknown works by P. D. Q. Bach (1807–1742?), allegedly the youngest and the most deservedly obscure of Johann Sebastian Bach's many children. After the manuscripts for "The Hindenberg Concerto (A Popular Disaster)" and "The Goldbrick Variations" were noticed lining the bottom of birdcages, propping up short table legs, etc., it was only a matter of time before Prof. Schickele would herald the discovery of a P. D. Q. Bach "bluegrass cantata," found stopping up a methane leak in a Kentucky coal mine.

Although classical music fans will probably get the most laughs out of this recording, bluegrassers will enjoy hearing some accomplished pickers (Bill Keith, banjo; Eric Weissberg, mandolin; Happy Traum, guitar) making music under the decidedly bent baton of Maestro Schickele.

High point: the famous Lester Flatt bluegrass guitar run in the key of G, perfectly executed by the flute section.

SEVEN

KENTUCKY FRIED AND FINGER PICKIN' GOOD

The Osborne Brothers

In the summertime I'd work—I would have to plow and disc and stuff like that because Dad was still working at the National Cash Register Company. . . . At night I'd get the banjo and go out on the back porch and just play until 3:00 or 4:00 in the morning. Then I'd run upstairs and jump into bed 'cause when Dad came in he'd always open the door and there I'd be just a-sleeping, so he didn't know I'd been playing the banjo all night. I was only getting two hours of sleep a night but I was learning to pick that banjo.

—Sonny Osborne to interviewer Bill Emerson

At one stage in their careers, Bobby and Sonny Osborne came to be regarded as the bad boys of bluegrass. Certainly they were high-profile rebels who went their own way with countrified musical experiments, marching to the beat of a different drummer and even adding a drummer, all of which infuriated bluegrass traditionalists.

But if anybody had a right to take or discard what they wanted from the bluegrass idiom, it was Bob and Sonny: Their very lives are almost a microcosm of bluegrass history.

Their family came from the Appalachian mountains of Kentucky. They moved to Dayton, Ohio, in the mid-1940s when their father sought factory work. They loved the country music that reminded them of home. As a teenager Bobby, the elder of the sons, formed a band and dreamed of being a star on the Grand Ole Opry.

Bobby really got into bluegrass after teaming with a hot banjo player named Larry Richardson. He developed considerable powers as a tenor vocalist (and later as a mandolinist, although he started out playing guitar). He and Richardson sought music careers, first on a local radio station, then in West Virginia, where they became members of the Lonesome Pine Fiddlers. The outfit had been something of an old-timey string band which (according to one story) took its name from a popular novel about southern life, *Trail of the Lonesome Pine*. The band featured various members of the Cline clan—Ezra and his nephews Charlie and Curly Ray, all destined to become great bluegrass sidemen. Under the influence of Osborne and Richardson (who soon went off to play in other bands), the Lonesome Pine Fiddlers became one of the truly legendary bluegrass bands that proliferated in the 1950s.

Meanwhile younger brother Sonny Osborne had become a decent banjo player and was getting better every day. Sonny saw Bill Monroe's band in concert and became friendly with his then-lead singer Jimmy Martin. Later, while only a fourteen-year-old, Sonny would himself play and record with Monroe.

The brothers played in different bands until they linked up as an act and began a series of short-lived but wonderful collaborations with great lead singers: Jimmy Martin, Charlie Bailey (formerly of the Bailey Brothers), and Red Allen. With Allen, who like the Osbornes was a product of the midwestern school of bluegrass bar bands and accompanying hard knocks, the Osbornes in 1956 won a contract with MGM Records and a spot on the prestigious "Jamboree" country music show on WWVA radio, Wheeling, West Virginia.

The smooth and stunningly powerful trio singing of the Osbornes and Red Allen has become the stuff of legend. But Red left in 1958 to play what was already becoming the "traditional" style of bluegrass while the Osbornes continued their innovations. Their sound became admittedly more "commercial" as the drums and occasional pedal steel guitars they used in the studio appealed to the larger country-and-western audience. This landed them a deal with Decca Records (now known as MCA and at the time very powerful in the country music field), and then they realized Bobby's childhood dream when they were invited to join the Grand Ole Opry.

The unique Osborne Brothers sound is defined by several important factors: The brothers harmonize well and select third members of their trio who blend well with them; these harmonies soar into turns and nuances as tightly and powerfully as a U.S. Air Force precision jet fighter flying team; the harmonies are stacked so that Bobby's high tenor lead stays on top with a high baritone underneath and under that a low tenor (a strategy which has also proven quite effective in blending female and male voices in bluegrass); finally, Bob and Sonny are crackerjack instrumentalists who play in a hard-driving, crisp, stacatto style backed by a smooth rhythm section. (Rhythm guitarists with the Osborne Brothers are generally instructed to play a straight up and down strumming rhythm without the punctuating runs used by most bluegrass guitarists.)

And there's the great material. The Osbornes have contributed several classics to the parking-lot jam-session repertoire, notably "Rocky Top" (composed by Felice and Boudleaux Bryant, who, incidentally, wrote numerous other country and pop hits including "Bye Bye Love" for the Everly Brothers).

In the early 1970s, the Osbornes riled many die-hard bluegrass fans by directly amplifying their instruments for on-stage performances. Sonny defended the decision with the same passion he brought to his music, pointing out that the pickups in their instruments simply increased volume with minimal distortion of the acoustic sound. The idea, he explained, was simply to be heard and not put audiences to sleep when they appeared on shows opposite heavily amplified country-and-western bands.

Sonny, in fact, could be as stubborn and proudly individualistic as his old boss. One year in the late 1960s when the Osborne

Brothers were invited to Bill Monroe's major festival in Bean Blossom, Indiana, an intermediary told the brothers, "Bill would like you to leave your amplifiers home." To which Sonny replied, "Then you tell Bill to leave his pick home, 'cause it's all just a matter of amplification!" The Osbornes missed Bean Blossom that year, although they were a hit on the rest of the circuit. Sonny, meanwhile, was so happy with the clear acoustic sound he got out of the pickup mounted inside his banjo that he literally installed a lock on his resonator so no one could get a peek inside and steal his design.

But the Osbornes were admired by and, in turn, sympathetic to the new breed of adventurous "newgrassers." Maybe it was because they were such upstarts themselves that the young, long-haired, Yankee superpickers could relate to them. (Goateed and solidly built, Sonny looks less like your typical bluegrass banjo picker and more like he should be singing villainous roles in Italian operas.)

And of late the Osborne Brothers have had something else in common with the rebellious newgrassers: They've reconfirmed their love for the Monroe-style sound, first by cutting some well-received albums of "essential" bluegrass with Mac Wiseman on the CMH label and more recently by recording *Hillbilly Fever*, a CD that not only contains some great straight bluegrass but also features as its cover art an absolutely wonderful takeoff on the cover of Flatt and Scruggs' classic Mercury album *Country Music* (right down to dobro ace Josh Graves reprising his role in the lower right-hand corner of the band picture).

As of this writing, many of the Osbornes' best-loved recordings from their Decca/MCA years are out of print, although they have re-recorded some of these hits for the CMH label, allowing us to go up on "Rocky Top" once more.

Despite their forays into country-and-western, the Osborne Brothers remain a bluegrass phenomenon, one of those rare acts that have contributed to both quintessential bluegrass and the cutting edge of progressive 'grass.

The Osborne Brothers. *Country Pickin' and Hillside Singin'*, **HAT-3129 (with Red Allen; MGM sessions)**

————. *Yesterday, Today and the Osborne Brothers,* Decca/MCA 74993 (one side, remakes of classic bluegrass; the flip side, country-and-western-style music)

————. *From Rocky Top to Muddy Bottom,* CMH 9008

————. *Hillbilly Fever,* CMH 6269

———— and Mac Wiseman. *The Essential Bluegrass Album,* CMH 9016

EIGHT

CROSSING OVER

Jim and Jesse McReynolds

I just knew I could if I worked at it.
—Jesse McReynolds, when asked by interviewer Jack
Tottle how he decided that a mandolin picker could
move a flatpick as fast as a banjo player moves three
fingerpicks

Audiences at the 1963 Newport (Rhode Island) Folk Festival were in for several surprises: that the bluegrass and old-time country music being featured that year wasn't squawky hillbilly stuff but, by and large, real folk music; that in the hands of a guitar master like Doc Watson, the flatpick wasn't just for the simple strumming of chords; and that the mandolin could have the quality, impact, and even the speed of three-finger-style 5-string banjo picking.

Proving the latter point on such show pieces as "Dill Pickle Rag" and "She Left Me Standing on the Mountain" was Jesse McReynolds, who with his guitarist brother headed up Jim and Jesse and the Virginia Boys.

The seemingly eternally youthful McReynolds brothers from Coeburn, Virginia (a tenor's note from the Stanleys' birthplace) are actually bluegrass veterans who started out on record in the early 1950s as a brother guitar/mandolin duet supplemented by bass. Although they knew and loved the bluegrass music of Monroe and the Stanleys, early vocal influences came from the smooth approach to "cowboy" music by the Sons of the Pioneers and from the immortal country duet of the Louvin Brothers (Charlie and Ira). Jim and Jesse later recorded Louvin Brothers songs as part of a tribute album, and several of these numbers—"When I Stop Dreaming," "Cash on the Barrelhead" and "Are You Missing Me?"—became central to the McReynolds repertoire.

The lovely vocal blend of Jim and Jesse exhibited both power and grace. It would have been enough to bring them to popularity. But they had something extra.

And what the initially banjoless brothers had was a catchy banjo-type sound thanks to Jesse's cross-picking on the mandolin. Just as a Scruggs-style banjo player would play in thumb-forefinger-middle finger (or thumb-middle-fore) combinations, Jesse played rapid-fire down-up-up patterns with his flatpick. Once he had it perfected, this innovative musician could match speed with the swift Scruggs-style banjo pickers hired as part of the brothers' shift into bluegrass when forming their Virginia Boys band. (In the studio, Jesse will often lower the "action" of his instrument—the distance between the strings and the fingerboard, determined by the adjustable string bridge—use a lighter pick, and have the volume boosted so he can play light and fast. But it hardly seems necessary, as he has been able to recreate the speed and precision of his recorded solos on stage with the higher and louder mandolin setup.)

They've also had their share of top sidemen over the years, including fiddlers Vassar Clements and Tommy Jackson and banjoists Allen Shelton and Bobby Thompson. (Thompson created a style of straight melody line playing, simultaneous with but independent of the better-known style developed by New England native Bill Keith.) And like most other top bluegrass bands, Jim and Jesse have gone through several stages and record contracts in their career. After some early duet recordings on the Kentucky label, they recorded some of their best full bluegrass for Capitol, Starday and Epic.

But like the Osborne Brothers, Jim and Jesse raised eyebrows and disappointments among bluegrassers in the late 1960s when, as members of the Grand Ole Opry, they shifted to a more consciously Nashville sound with pedal steel, electric bass, and drums. Unlike the Osbornes, they went about it quietly and also used standard acoustic instrumentation for bluegrass festival performances. Their musical experiments of this era were quite interesting (notably their album of Chuck Berry rhythm-and-blues/rock-and-roll classics, *Berry Pickin' in the Country*), and they retained their love of train songs.

Jim and Jesse remain active, recording self-produced bluegrass albums that have been well received by their old fans. Some of these feature the versatile Jesse doubling on fiddle and, as always, the strong but soothing tenor of his brother Jim.

An interesting footnote to Virginia Boys history: When guitarist Robby Krieger of the Doors rock band penned the song "Running Blue," he wanted to combine country and rhythm-and-blues passages in the recorded version. The R&B part was easy. The Doors were recording their *Soft Parade* album for Elektra with full horn sections. Through some networking, Krieger linked up with Jesse McReynolds and then–Virginia Boys fiddler Jimmy Buchanan, who traveled to Los Angeles. Jesse told me he enjoyed working with Krieger and the other instrumentalists but didn't get to meet Jim Morrison: The Doors' celebrated Dionysian lead singer was not at the studio that day but overdubbed his vocals later.

Every time I see Jesse McReynolds, I tell him he was the best darn mandolin picker the Doors ever had, no question. He always grins. And why not? Presumably the Doors and the L.A. studio musicians were just as blown away by his cross-picking as the folkies at Newport had been.

Jim and Jesse and the Virginia Boys. *Classic Recordings,* **BCD-15635 (the Capitol sessions)**

———. *Bluegrass and More,* **Bear 15716 (the Epic and Columbia sessions)**

———. *Berry Pickin' in the Country,* **P-18422**

————. *In the Tradition,* **Rounder 0234**

————. *Music among Friends,* **Rounder 0279**

The Long Steel Rails and the Short Cross Ties

Railroads . . . are positively the greatest blessing that the ages have wrought out for us. They give us wings. They annihilate the toil and dust of pilgrimage, they spiritualize travel!

—Nathaniel Hawthorne, The House of Seven Gables

And railroads have provided the subjects or the settings for a trainyard of great bluegrass songs.

Rail travel was not as important a form of transportation for bluegrass musicians in the early days as it was for their jazz colleagues. The latter went primarily from city to big city; bluegrass venues were in both town and country, necessitating car and bus travel. But the train as symbol demanded the same allegiance from bluegrassers as it had from their folk and old-time predecessors.

The train was powerful, exhilarating (any version of Erwin Rouse's classic fiddle tune "Orange Blossom Special" gives players a chance to imitate not only the drive of the wheels but the whistle, the bell, and the hiss of the airbrakes). The train promised travel and change. Not all this change was pleasant, with its threat of desertion on the platform ("The Train That Carried My Girl from Town"). Like a drug, it could swallow you up ("Midnight Train," a Stanley Brothers standard).

Jimmie Rodgers, the Yodeling Brakeman who was a real railroad worker and later country music's first superstar, recorded numerous train songs. "Waiting for a Train" is one of the best as you start rooting for the hero, who admits to being a hobo.

"Life's Railway to Heaven" is a gospel song that uses the train system metaphorically. "The Wreck of the Old 97" is in the popular "event song" genre of early country music. Other event songs were written about dramas as local as school bus crashes and as internationally known as the sinking of the Titanic. The wreck in question was the crash of the Fast Mail of the Southern Railway on September 27, 1903, on its regular run between Monroe and Spencer, Virginia, in which engineer Joseph A. (Steve) Broady and 12 others died. The original author of the words to this song is not known for certain. But one recording in the early 1920s sold six million copies, an incredible number for that or any day.

"The Wreck of the Old 97"—at least its melody—got back on the charts in the 1950s when it was used as the basis of a local song turned national hit that protested fare increases on the Boston Metropolitan Transit Authority subways. The plot of "Charlie on the MTA" has the hapless protagonist, like a latter day Flying Dutchman, unable to make his transfer and doomed to stay on the train because he is short a nickel.

It seemed as if Canadian folk-rocker Gordon Lightfoot wrote the epitaph to folkie train songs when he observed in his song "Early Morning Rain" that you can't jump a jet plane like you can a freight train. But the lure is always there.

NINE

THE CLASSIC
SOUTHERN SOUND

It is the best of all trades to make songs, and the second best
to sing them.
—Hillaire Belloc, British poet and essayist

There are unsung heroes and there are undersung heroes who
sing great. Bluegrass has produced many of the latter. Beneath
the pantheon of bluegrass gods sit the saints who ensured the triumph of the bluegrass form. Many of these are the great gui-
tarist/vocalists.

Foremost among them are singers like Mac Wiseman, the
well-named "Voice with a Heart," who can swing the ends of his
lines yet possesses such a mellowness that you can only sit back,
relax, and wonder why bluegrass singing is stereotyped as nasal
and twangy. Wiseman has the distinction of having recorded
with Monroe and Flatt and Scruggs and having worked on some
memorable albums with the Osborne Brothers when those
beloved prodigals returned to the bluegrass fold.

Clyde Moody, the first guitarist/singer to record with the Blue
Grass Boys, is interesting as a pioneer with an authentic present-
at-the-creation voice. Jim Eanes, a member of the famed Blue
Ridge Entertainers country band, who has also done on-stage

5. Mac Wiseman (courtesy of Mac Wiseman Enterprises).

stints with Monroe, is a gentleman with a country voice that does well with bluegrass material. Frank "Hylo" Brown (who got the nickname for his ability to jump easily back and forth from a baritone to a high tenor range) recorded pop country music backed by vocal choruses in the 1950s. But he also played as a bluegrass sideman (on Flatt and Scruggs sessions) and recorded as a bluegrass-style solo artist before the mode was recognized as a separate form of country music. Hylo Brown's voice quality and phrasings deserve a wider audience today.

Other vocalists have trained with the masters of the first generation and now come into their own. Two deserve special mention: Del McCoury and Larry Sparks.

McCoury was in a classic mid-1960s version of the Blue Grass

6. The Del McCoury Band (photo by Jim McGuire).

Boys and then went his own way. His voice is consistently strong and tempered, the kind of bluegrass voice that is drawn effortlessly from the instrumental ensemble around it like a sword from a scabbard. Yet McCoury is blessed with a genuineness in his delivery that evokes an empathetic reaction in his listeners.

Sparks has earned the gratitude of a generation of bluegrass fans as being the man who helped save the Stanley sound. After Carter's death it seemed that Ralph could never approach the powerful lonesome mountain quality once the brothers' trademark. Sparks was a confident, ready replacement who had fully absorbed Carter's style until it was second nature, and his talents assured a seamless transition to a new edition of the Clinch Mountain Boys. Since founding his own band, Sparks has emerged as his own singer with a quiet passion to his deliveries, like a mountain wind coaxing the coals of a campfire into life.

There are numerous other great vocalists, such as Red Allen, who exude a raw and captivating power, and there are others, like Bill Harrell and Charlie Waller, who belie the notion that bluegrass singing is shrill hillbillyizing. Their roles in the development of bluegrass will be considered in the next chapter.

Hylo Brown. *Hylo Brown and The Timberlines 1954–1960,* **Bear Family 15572**

Jim Eanes and the Shenandoah Valley Boys. *Classic Bluegrass,* **Rebel 1116**

———. *Log Cabin in the Lane,* **HT 388**

Bill Harrell and the Virginians. *Classic Bluegrass,* **Rebel 1113**

———. *After the Sunrise,* **Rebel 1685**

Del McCoury. *Livin' on the Mountain,* **Rebel 1709**

———. *Don't Stop the Music,* **Rounder 0245**

———. *Lonesome Side of Town,* **Rounder 0292**

———. *A Deeper Shade of Blue,* **Rounder 0303**

Clyde Moody. *White House Blues,* **Rebel 1672**

Charlie Moore. *The Fiddler,* **Old Homestead**

Larry Sparks and the Lonesome Ramblers. *John Deere Tractor,* **Rebel 1597**

————. *Classic Recordings,* **Rebel 1107**
————. *Travelin',* **Rebel 1700**
Mac Wiseman. *Early Dot Recordings,* **County 113**
————. *Classic Bluegrass,* **Rebel 1108**
————. *Grassroots to Bluegrass,* **CMH 9041**
————. *The Mac Wiseman Story,* **CMH 9001 (with the excellent Shenandoah Cutups backup band)**

The Great Sidemen

I've never known a musician who regretted being one.
—Virgil Thomson, American composer and critic

As with the great bluegrass singer/guitarists, many instrumentalists have made such a mark on bluegrass in specific ways that I'm considering them elsewhere. But if you really want to have fun, get to know some of the less celebrated—but no less great—bluegrass acts. Sure, everybody idolizes Bill Monroe and is awed by the Foggy Mountain Boys, but who's your favorite sideman or festival opening act?

Curly Seckler sang truly heroic tenor on many of Flatt and Scruggs' most famous recordings and deserves any bit of the spotlight that shines on him. Charlie, Ezra, and Curly Ray Cline and the Goins Brothers were at various times members of the Lonesome Pine Fiddlers, an old-timey band that made the transition to bluegrass in the 1950s and recorded some absolutely great stuff in the process.

J. D. Crowe, the former Jimmy Martin sideman whose driving banjo defined the Sunny Mountain Boys sound, went on to found the New South, famed for its laser-focused harmonies and frightening instrumental precision. (Members have included such talents as Doyle Lawson, Tony Rice, Larry Rice, Ricky Skaggs, and Jimmy Gaudreau.) Any band featuring Larry Richardson, Raymond Fairchild, or Curtis McPeake has been known for no-nonsense banjo-driven bluegrass.

The Dixie Gentlemen and the Shenandoah Cutups have sometimes been better known (and more frequently recorded) as

7. Larry Sparks (courtesy of Rebel Records).

backup bands to free-agent lead vocalists. The Pinnacle Boys have been featuring a potent mix of smooth Louvin Brothers–style harmonies and twin fiddles playing in tight harmony. Acts such as Red Cravens and the Bray Brothers (formerly known as the Bluegrass Gentlemen) or Curtis Blackwell and the Dixie Bluegrass Boys are bands who have been known to be scheduled in the early "warmup" positions at major bluegrass festivals only to steal the show and make themselves literally the "tough act to follow."

A true bluegrass lover develops his/her ear for these wonderful sounds as a wine connoisseur develops a palate for rare, fine wines.

Curtis Blackwell and the Dixie Bluegrass Boys. *On and On,* **Atteiram 1685**

Church Brothers. *The Early Days Of Bluegrass Vol. 8,* **Rounder 1020**

Charlie Cline and the Lonesome Pine Fiddlers. *For Crying Out Loud,* **Atteiram API-CD-1683**

Red Cravens and the Bray Brothers. *419 West Main,* **Rounder 0015**

J. D. Crowe and the New South. *J. D. Crowe and the New South,* **Rounder 0044 (with Tony Rice, Ricky Skaggs, and Jerry Douglas)**

———. *You Can Share My Blanket,* **Rounder 0096 (with Tony and Larry Rice)**

Dixie Gentlemen. *Take Me Back to Dixie,* **Rural Rhythm 3016**

Raymond Fairchild and Arthur Smith. *Swinging on the Swinging Bridge,* **CMH 6271**

Goins Brothers. *Still Goin' Strong,* **Hay Holler Harvest 501**

Good Ol' Boys. *Pistol Packin' Mama,* **Grateful Dead Records 40122 (with Don Reno, Chubby Wise, Frank Wakefield, and Dave Nelson)**

The Lonesome Pine Fiddlers. *Windy Mountain,* **Copper 501**

The Pinnacle Boys. *The Pinnacle Boys,* **Rounder 0049 (Louvin harmonies and Monroe-style twin fiddles)**

Larry Richardson and Red Barker. *Larry Richardson, Red Barker and the Blue Ridge Boys,* **County 702**

Curly Seckler and Willis Spears. *A Tribute to Lester Flatt,* **Rebel 4301**

Keith Whitley and Ricky Skaggs. *Second Generation Bluegrass,* **Rebel 1504**

Turn Up Your Radio Dials!

Some of the best bluegrass ever—and perhaps the most beloved—was featured in radio broadcasts of the 1940s and early '50s.

At the appointed hour, bands would burst over the airwaves with a few bars of a fast-paced theme song (usually a hot fiddle instrumental). Then the announcer would proffer welcomes and introduce the musicians. Such introductions were merely a formality: Everyone across the invisible realm of radio quickly became old friends as listeners, with just a twist of the dial, would invite their favorite performers into their kitchens, living rooms, and parlors. Band members would banter with each other, fill requests, and offer at least one gospel number in keeping with the traditional values of the day.

All this seems hopelessly quaint in today's world of Top-40 and album broadcasting formats, Arbitron ratings, and the Federal Communications Commission's incessant watchdog efforts to keep four-letter words out of the ether. But make no mistake: This was prime-time entertainment. Many of the shows were broadcast early in the morning or at the lunch hour, when tens of thousands of farm families and hired hands gathered around tables across the South, hungry for food and diversion in the midst of their hard lives.

One of the most famous bluegrass- and country-oriented radio shows, "Farm and Fun Time" on WCYB, Bristol, Tennessee, was directly aimed at this audience. No wonder the shows featured announcements of upcoming local appearances (schoolhouses being the usual concert venue in the rural regions) plus commercials for a variety of patent medicines.

Some of the music is truly unique, displaying both the discipline of a recording session and the spontaneity of a live show. The most popular bands couldn't always tour and make it back to their radio station base to appear live, so recordings were sometimes made on large-format half-hour discs for later broadcast. That's great for us, because a lot of wonderful moments were preserved. There was also some recording of shows during the early days of reel-to-reel audio tape. Such material occasionally shows up on independent bootleg albums.

So settle back, friends and neighbors, and enjoy. . . .

Jim and Jesse and the Virginia Boys. *Radio Shows,* **OD 49812**

Charlie Monroe. *Vintage Radio,* **Rebel 4302**

Stanley Brothers. *On WCYB Farm and Fun Time,* **Rebel 855**

———. *On Radio,* **Rebel 1115**

Tennessee Hilltoppers. *On WCYB Farm and Fun Time,* **Heartland 504**

Various artists. *Live Again! WCYB Bristol Farm and Fun Time,* **Rebel 854 (Featuring Carl and J. P. Sauceman, Flatt and Scruggs, Mac Wiseman, the Stanley Brothers)**

Various artists. *Old-Time Music on the Radio,* **Rounder 0331**

TEN

ACROSS THE MASON-DIXON LINE

A Capital Sound, the Heartfelt Heartland, Yankee Explorers, and the Way-out West

The people were hungry for music, you see.
— Bill Monroe to the author

The Country Gentlemen, the Seldom Scene, and D. C. Grass

It's not surprising that the nation's capital, geographically rubbing against the North and South, has produced a bluegrass notable for its northern-style innovation and solid southern sensibilities.

Consider in particular the Country Gentlemen and the Seldom Scene.

At the time the original Country Gentlemen band was formed in 1957—as a pickup band to play at the last minute at a

Washington-area bar—no one could predict how influential and downright excellent this ensemble would become. Its first classic lineup was fronted by singer/guitarist Charlie Waller, a performer greatly influenced by Hank "The Singing Ranger" Snow, the duo of Johnny and Jack, and other country songsters. On mandolin and singing tenor was John Duffey, the son of an opera singer. Eddie Adcock, an experienced bluegrass banjo picker, contributed near-perfect baritone parts to the trio harmonies. One admirer (Mitch Jayne of the Dillards) caught the band on stage at the Shamrock Inn and later declared that they moved and fit and sang as smoothly around a microphone as the parts in a well-oiled Browning slide-action shotgun.

But what really blew away bluegrass audiences was the explosive chemistry between the irrepressible Adcock and the domineering Duffey. The imposing mandolinist and the wiry banjoist pushed each other to greater creative heights and improvisational fancies, with the genial Waller and a series of serious bass players being the perfect counterbalance to the escalating antics of their partners. Some Country Gentlemen routines are now legendary, particularly the ego-tripping musical oneupmanship on "Dueling Banjos" that would erupt into comic warfare between Duffey and Adcock.

The Washington and Baltimore areas had an active folk, country, and bluegrass scene at this time. (They still do. One artist whose success as a capital city music maker was recently followed by national stardom is country singer Mary Chapin Carpenter.) Several performers made major contributions to bluegrass music while working in the region.

There was Buzz Busby, one of the cult figures of early bluegrass. There was Jack Tottle, whose Lonesome River Boys traveled north in 1962 to make one of the first bluegrass albums ever recorded in New York. There was Bill Clifton, who championed the music of the Carter Family to folk audiences and who produced in 1963 what was probably the very first all-day, all-bluegrass music festival. There was the Stoneman Family, Appalachian transplants whose members included patriarch Ernest "Pop" Stoneman, whose career spanned the days of horn recordings to the era of full stereo sound; Roni Stoneman, later a banjo-

8. The classic Country Gentlemen: Charlie Waller, Eddie Adcock,
Ed Ferris, and John Duffey (kneeling) (courtesy of Bluegrass Unlimited).

picking comedienne on the *Hee Haw* television show; and Scotty
Stoneman, one of the most memorable fiddle players who ever
laid bow to string. There was Bill Harrell, a singer of traditional
bluegrass who had become a resident of the suburbs in Maryland. And later there was Cliff Waldron and the New Shades of
Grass who would build successfully on what the Country Gentlemen had started.

But the Gents were unique. Their repertoire included straight
bluegrass tunes, big band instrumentals arranged for banjo, guitar, and mandolin, plus folk ballads that went beyond simple expressions of love or heartbreak to tell a complete and compelling
story. (The band started hitting its stride during the major folk
music revival and that helped gain them exposure on the college
circuit.) They proved that, as great as Monroe, the Stanley Brothers, and Flatt and Scruggs were, the bluegrass they had championed could encompass other musical genres and be enhanced by
them.

To give you an idea of how far ahead of their time these guys
were: In 1961 the band recorded "Silence or Tears," a good old
tug-at-your-heart country number that took its lyrics from Byron's poem "When We Two Parted." The adventurous arrangement by bassist Tom Gray and his friend Jerry Stuart provided
for the words to be sung slowly and movingly while the instruments snapped along at exactly double tempo.

Hot pickers in New York would one day firmly establish an alternative school of bluegrass and a band from Louisville would
give it a name; but many people feel that what we now call "newgrass" was first performed in the Shamrock Inn, Birchmere, and
other clubs in our nation's capital.

Now established as one of the all-time great bluegrass bands,
the Gentlemen sound still features the mellow voice of Charlie
Waller. The band has gone through numerous personal changes
but these have only served to benefit both D. C.-area and American bluegrass. Banjo players Bill Emerson (who actually helped
organize the first Gents gig) and James Bailey did turns with the
band, as did the mandolinists Jimmy Gaudreau and Doyle Lawson. Ricky Skaggs, who had first come to fame as a teenager touring with Ralph Stanley, played fiddle with the Gents en route to

his present country music superstardom. The band was also the first major showcase for the awesome talents of Jerry "Flux" Douglas, now bluegrass music's most popular dobro player.

Adcock has fronted several of his own progressive 'grass ensembles since his days with the Gentlemen, and Gaudreau has been a mainstay of several more. Lawson now heads Quicksilver, which excels in both gospel music and secular bluegrass. After being slightly wounded in a shooting incident at a bar in the early 1970s, Emerson enlisted in the Navy and took the helm of its Country Currents band. He has since retired from the service, occasionally recording and performing with a series of singer/songwriter partners.

9. The Seldom Scene today: Moondi Klein, John Duffey, T. Michael Coleman, Ben Eldridge and Mike Auldridge (seated) (courtesy of Keith Case Associates).

Duffey retired from performing in 1969 to devote full time to being a luthier (instrument maker). That didn't last long. He was soon having weekly picking-and-singing sessions with a group of outstanding musicians who also held interesting jobs: John Starling (guitar/physician), Mike Auldridge (dobro/commercial artist), Ben Eldridge (banjo/mathematician), and Tom Gray (bass/National Geographic cartographer). Their careers, they reasoned, wouldn't allow them to appear on stage often, so they named themselves the Seldom Scene.

That didn't last long either; no musicians associated with John Duffey will ever become wallflowers in the garden of bluegrass. Over the years the Seldom Scene has played a major role in introducing bluegrass to new audiences: with triumphant appearances at folk festivals, through its stirring rendition of "Hail to the Redskins" at R.F.K. Stadium, via collaborations with folk/pop divas Linda Ronstadt and Emmy Lou Harris, but mostly because of its compelling and often dramatic music. Whether it's a novelty number, a gospel quartet, a dreamy ballad, or a rip-snorting banjo piece, almost everything this band turns its talents to becomes mini-theater.

The "Scene" was well named after all.

The Eddie Adcock Band. *Dixie Fried,* **CMH 6270**

Bill Clifton. *The Early Years, 1957–1958,* **Rounder 1021**

———. *Where the Rainbow Finds Its End,* **Elf 102**

———. *Blue Ridge Mountain Bluegrass,* **Elf 501 (with guests John Duffey, Mike Seeger, Tommy Jackson, Gordon Terry, Ralph Stanley, and Curly Lambert)**

Country Gentlemen. *Nashville Jail,* **CCCD 0111 (Waller, Duffey, Adcock, Gray)**

———. *Bringing Mary Home,* **Rebel 1478 (Waller, Duffey, Adcock, Gray)**

———. *Folk Songs and Bluegrass,* **Smithsonian/Folkways 40022 (Waller, Duffey, Adcock, Gray)**

———. *Sound Off,* **Rebel 1501 (Waller, Emerson, Gaudreau, and Yates)**

————. *The Award Winning Country Gentlemen,* Rebel 1506 (Waller, Emerson, Lawson, and Yates)

————. *Classic Country Gents Reunion,* Sugar Hill 3772 (Waller, Duffey, Adcock, Gray)

————. *New Horizon,* Rebel 1699 (with guests Glen Duncan, Gene Wooten and Randall Hylton)

Bill Emerson. *Home of the Red Fox,* Rebel 1651

Doyle Lawson and Quicksilver. *Pressing On Regardless,* Brent 5304

Leon Morris and Buzz Busby. *Honky Tonk Bluegrass,* Rounder 0031

Seldom Scene. *Act I,* Rebel 1511

————. *Act II,* Rebel 1520

————. *Act III,* Rebel 1528

————. *Live at the Cellar Door,* Rebel 1103

————. *20th Anniversary Concert,* Sugar Hill 2501/2 (with guest Emmy Lou Harris)

————. *Scenic Roots,* Sugar Hill 3785

————. *Like We Used to Be,* Sugar Hill 3822

John Starling. *Long Time Gone,* Sugar Hill 3714

Stoneman Family. *Cuttin' the Grass,* CMH 9005

Charlie Waller and Randall Hylton. *The Singer and the Songster,* Rebel 1679

Red Allen, Earl Taylor, and Heartfelt Bluegrass in the Heartland

High mountains are a feeling, but
the hum of human cities torture.
                    —Lord Byron, English poet

As was noted earlier, musicologists and folklorists have made a strong case that country music in general and bluegrass in particular developed as a nostalgic home link for displaced southerners working in northern and midwestern factories. (Rural African-American blues became big city rhythm-and-blues in much the same way.) That was true during initial migrations in the 1920s and 1930s, and it remained true in the 1950s and '60s.

As workers continued to migrate from the South to the factories of Ohio, Michigan, and Illinois, bluegrass was there to entertain them.

But there is musical interest in this and not some dry sociology. Red Allen, Earl Taylor, Charlie Moore, Bill Napier, and others helped define a distinctive Midwest bluegrass sound. It was by turns as sunny as the country music parks and as dark as the bars in which it was performed.

There is some excellent home-grown midwestern bluegrass to

10. Vernon McIntyre's Appalachian Grass (photo by Mark Alexander).

be heard today. Minnesota's version has grown in parallel to its active folk scene: One of the best is Stony Lonesome, with guest appearances on Minnesota Public Radio's nationally syndicated "A Prairie Home Companion." Way down the Mississippi, there's a Louisiana version that, as you might expect, has Cajun influences. (What you might not expect is the influence bluegrass, especially early Bill Monroe, has had on Cajun and Zydeco. The lonesome slides up from flatted thirds on some waltz numbers have—to my ears at least—an unmistakable bluegrass echo.)

Such veteran midwestern bands as Boys from Indiana, Mac Martin and the Dixie Travelers, and Vern McIntyre's Appalachian Grass are perennial favorites on the bluegrass festival circuit. By keeping the down-to-basics style of bluegrass alive and well, in a real sense these bands have widened the trail for the Johnson Mountain Boys and other exponents of the "new traditionalism" in today's bluegrass.

Many of the musicians who became identified with Midwestern bluegrass made their marks elsewhere too. Two notable examples were Taylor and Allen: both were for a time mainstays of Washington bluegrass. And both, incidentally, were Foggy Mountain Boys in the mid-1960s: Taylor doubled on mandolin and harmonica, and Allen was pressed into service when ill health temporarily took Lester Flatt off the road. It would be an interesting scholarly exercise someday to chart all the personnel relations among classic bluegrass bands, but I fear the software and mainframe memory does not yet exist to even create a database on all the fiddlers who have worked with Bill Monroe. . . .

Earl Taylor has other claims to fame. Although not well known to new listeners, he was a major figure in his time, the first bluegrasser to land a recording contract with a major label (United Artists) that did not otherwise specialize in country music. And in 1959 Taylor and his Stoney Mountain Boys became the first bluegrass band to perform at Carnegie Hall (under the auspices of folklorist Alan Lomax), beating the time of the Country Gentlemen (1961) and Flatt and Scruggs (1962).

Allen was hardly uncomfortable in the bar setting. He was a man known to appreciate song, female companionship, and refreshment, not necessarily in that order. But he was a bluegrass

singing talent of the first order. His raw, nasal style might strike
some as the stereotype of a bluegrass singer, but he was the genuine article and one of the best to assay the high lonesome sound.
The Osborne Brothers were only two of the great talents with
whom Red melded his own gifts. His trio with Doyle Lawson
and J. D. Crowe was also quite awesome, and their picking easily rivaled that of the Osbornes. A later edition of the Kentuckians matched Red with two highly unlikely collaborators: Bill
Keith, a brilliant and analytical New Englander who had perfected a melodic style of banjo picking, and Frank Wakefield, a
mad genius of the mandolin who had totally mastered the Monroe style and gone on to create music that was as unabashedly
maniacal as one of his own grins.

Both Allen and Taylor are gone but some of their music has
been continued in reissues. The same is true of Charlie Moore,
whose unhurried style added to the power of his music. Other
Midwest bluegrass veterans such as Bill Napier and Larry Taylor continue to be appreciated.

Hopefully, more will be. As much as we idealize the green and
rolling hills of West Virginia, it was nearby in the tough and
smoky bars of Ohio, Indiana, and Illinois that one of the most authentic bluegrass styles developed.

**Red Allen, David Grisman, Herb Pederson, Jim Buchanan,
and James Kerwin, with Jerry Garcia.** *Bluegrass Reunion,*
Acoustic Disc 4

The Boys From Indiana. *Touchin' Home,* **Rebel 1695**

J. D. Crowe. *Bluegrass Holiday,* **Rebel 1598 (featuring Red
Allen and Doyle Lawson)**

Louisiana Honeydrippers. *Louisiana Bluegrass,* **Prestige International 13035**

Mac Martin and the Dixie Travelers. *Travelers' Portrait,* **Old
Homestead 90195**

Charlie Moore. *The Fiddler,* **Old Homestead 90052**

Bill Napier. *Hillbilly Fever,* **Old Homestead 80059**

———— **and Larry Taylor.** *A Country Boy's Life,* **Old Homestead
80076**

Smith Brothers. *The Grass Section,* Redclay 111

Special Consensus. *Hey, Y'All,* Turquoise 5076

Stony Lonesome. *Blue Heartache,* Red House 51

Earl Taylor and His Stoney Mountain Boys. *Folk Songs from the Blue Grass,* United Artists 3049

————. *Bluegrass Touch,* Vetco 3017

Various artists. *The Minnesota Album,* Minnesota Bluegrass and Old Time Music Association 101

Heartache, Country-Western and Bluegrass Style
An Unscientific Comparative Study

Question: What happens when you play a country-and-western record backwards?

Answer: You get your truck back, you get your job back, you sober up, and you get your girl back.

Okay, the idea is not to mock country music (which has gotten the last laugh on critics by becoming the most popular music in America today). But the protagonists of your average country and bluegrass songs do react very differently to having their hearts broken.

While the jilted anti-hero of a three-minute country ode might sing "I'm sitting on a barstool beneath the flashing neon sign trying to drink you off my mind before I have to roll that big rig to Austin," his bluegrass counterpart will be "sitting away up on a windy mountain beneath the lonesome pines, thinking of you and the days that used to be."

Lonely but not depressed, wounded but still proud, down but not out—the spirit is essential to bluegrass and probably has much to do with the life of founder Bill Monroe, who never smoked nor drank but who has been known to have a romance or two. The resulting joys and heartaches find autobiographical expression in what he terms his "true songs." When communicated by voices singing in a sharp-edged tenor range, this feeling has caused bluegrass to be rightly dubbed "The High Lonesome Sound."

An outstanding example of a lonesome "true song" is Monroe's "Letter from My Darling." Jimmy Martin, who was a member of the Blue Grass Boys in 1951 when this emotion-wrenching song was composed and who helped record it, once related the following story to me: Monroe had plans after a show to meet a woman with whom he was very involved. Upon calling for her at the hotel in which she was staying, he found the ultimate Dear John letter waiting for him: a missive with no forwarding address accusing him of being incapable of being faithful and signed "I love you so." Heartbroken, Monroe sat down and essentially wrote the song from the letter. Play his recording of it and you'll feel his pain swell forth from his mandolin solo and explode out of the speakers.

"Blue and Lonesome" (co-written by Monroe and country music legend Hank Williams backstage between shows during a tour) reflects the pain and resignation evoked in a spurned lover by a passing train when he recalls how his woman used that mode of transportation to leave him. The vocal in the chorus rises up to a high pitch like the train whistling by as the singer realizes his desire to do the same, just pack up and move on.

It's not surprising that bluegrass, with its Anglo-Celtic and African-American musical roots, would have such a strong blues tradition. (Interesting etymological point: the Elizabethans called depression "the blue devils," probably the source of our term "the blues.") And the "lonesome" feeling in bluegrass is not just the personal melancholia of one artist but something that strikes resonant chords in millions. For example, Monroe's "Kentucky Waltz," a lament of fleeting happiness and lost love, directly inspired Pee Wee King and Redd Stewart's composition "Tennessee Waltz," which, recorded by Peggy Lee and others, became a major national hit.

Such a feeling has become as much a part of bluegrass as its more high-profile hot picking. Flatt and Scruggs recorded the lonesome classic "Cora Is Gone," with its poignant references to whippoorwill calls and brush drifting down a river. The Stanleys gave us "The Lonesome River," with its frighteningly haunting high trio harmony in the chorus. ("The Banks of the Ohio" may have been the site of a famous love murder in folk music, but the Stanleys established riverbanks as a place of choice for bluegrass anti-heroes to mourn lost love.)

While modern songwriters have updated the lonesome theme in bluegrass, the best have managed to keep their protagonists out of the smoky honky-tonks frequented by the victims of love in Nashville songs. "Blue Virginia Blues" by Pete Goble and Leroy Drum (Bill Emerson and Pete Goble, Tennessee 1949, Webco 0123) ends with the desolate perspective of a man who has traveled to a distant town at the passionate urging of a lady, only to find no one waiting at the bus stop and her name not in the phone directory.

The bluegrass blues cut deep but clean.

The Yankees Are Coming

[I] walked in the door, and heard bluegrass for the first time in my entire life. The Charles River Valley Boys were on stage. At one point in my life, I had been a serious student of Bach, and now I heard bluegrass. It was country Bach! It had contrapuntal arrangements, all the fugal stuff. I just went completely insane.

—Paul Rothchild, Elektra Records executive, on visiting Club 47 in Cambridge, Massachusetts in 1962 (from Eric Von Schmidt and Jim Rooney, *Baby Let Me Follow You Down: The Illustrated Story of the Cambridge Folk Music Years,* second edition, Amherst: University of Massachusetts Press, 1994; originally published, Garden City N.Y.: Anchor Press/Doubleday, 1979 used by permission)

Numerous northerners were inspired to take up bluegrass during the great folk music revival of the 1960s. Some even went on to play in the Blue Grass Boys during the time when Bill Monroe's music was becoming revitalized. But it's safe to say they couldn't have done it without some musical missionaries.

Consider the case of Boston and nearby Cambridge, in Massachusetts.

The Lilly Brothers (Everett and Bea) of West Virginia had started out as a sibling mandolin/guitar duo influenced by the Monroe Brothers but developed their own sound. With a fellow West Virginian in the person of sturdy banjo picker Don Stover, they were soon finding fame and fortune playing bluegrass in Boston.

Well, maybe not fortune but at least a living performing at the Hillbilly Ranch, which like other bars in the downtown "combat zone" benefited from the then-active naval operations in Boston. On a Saturday night it was wall-to-wall sailors and hookers, with

the Lilly Brothers and Don Stover—aka the Confederate Mountaineers—picking bluegrass and ducking the occasional bottle
intended for someone else. The amount of blood spilled on a
busy evening was probably equivalent to that shed in your average southern rural roadhouse, so the boys must have felt at
least somewhat at home. When I finally got to play at the Hillbilly Ranch myself, this interesting era had long since ended. The
navy yard had closed, the crowds were sparse, there was a rent-
a-cop bouncer to keep order, and the ambulance was only called
once the whole night.

Joining the Lillys and Stover for an extended stretch in those
years was one Benjamin "Tex" Logan, a fiddler. Tex was from
Texas (as you probably have guessed). He was living in the area

11. Roger Sprung and Hal Wylie (photo by David Gahr).

because he was going to school across the river at the Massachu-setts Institute of Technology (as you probably would never have imagined) and went on to become a cult figure in bluegrass who would periodically emerge from his work on the mathematics of satellite communications at AT&T's Bell Labs to create incredi-ble waves and frequencies on the fiddle.

Having these guys in Boston (and having the "Hillbilly at Har-vard" radio show as a longtime institution on the Cambridge airwaves) was bound to have some effect. And it did.

By the early 1960s, a colony of first-rate bluegrassers was es-tablished in New England: Joe Val, an Italian-American man-dolin player with a tenor voice even Bill Monroe respected; Bob Siggins, a banjo-picking surgeon who joined with Val in forming

12. Peter Rowan (courtesy of Keith Case Associates).

the Charles River Valley Boys (named after the flow between Cambridge and Boston); Bill Keith, a protégé of Stover's (and already mentioned as a creator of the landmark melodic banjo style); and Keith's frequent musical partner Jim Rooney, a wry vocalist who had never gotten over Hank Williams (and who wrote *Bossmen,* which contained the first book-length biography of Bill Monroe).

Albums by Keith and Rooney and by the Charles River Valley Boys began popping up on the turntables of aspiring bluegrassers across the northeast. The high-water mark for the Charles River Valley Boys was an imaginative album of Lennon/McCartney songs, *Beatle Country,* made all the more successful by the fact that Joe Val (who was skeptical about the

13. Northern Lights (photo by David Spink).

project) played it completely straight, thus anchoring the results in bluegrass.

Cambridge, chockablock with colleges and coffee houses, had a vibrant folk music scene in those days. Audiences in greater Boston, unlike those in some parts of the country, didn't need well-footnoted articles to be told that bluegrass was a kind of folk music. It's not surprising that early on the Newport (Rhode Island) Folk Festival sought out and invited the very best bluegrass and old-timey musicians to appear. What is fortunate is that so many recordings from this period are readily available. (For Newport shows, see "Compilations" in chapter 15.)

Jack Tottle, who made his mark on bluegrass starting with his Washington days and continuing now as head of the Eastern Tennessee State bluegrass program, spent several years in Boston heading up the Tasty Licks band. Cancer stilled the great climbing voice and staccato mandolin of Joe Val, but his legacy continues in the playing of former sidemen, including Herb Applin and the Berkshire Mountain Bluegrass Boys.

Southern Rail, also based in the Boston area, has been recognized as a fresh new band in the traditional mode. Led by Jim Muller and Sharon Horovitch, the group showcases a great deal of self-written material.

Bluegrass continues to grow from the hills of Back Bay Boston (the Beacon Hill Billies) to the hills of Maine (the Kennebec Valley Boys, the Bluegrass Supply Company, and others). In between are Banjo Dan and the Mid-Nite Plowboys, Fred Pike and Sam Tidwell, longtime disc jockey Lee Moore ("The Coffee Drinking Night Hawk"), and other stalwarts of the New England/New York State bluegrass scene.

Without question, the greatest recent gift of Massachusetts bluegrass to the rest of the world has been Northern Lights. This phenomenal quartet of singing, picking, and songwriting talents keeps earning respect and building audiences nationwide; a true achievement for a band that was founded some degrees of latitude away from the Mason-Dixon line.

All this time you could also find bluegrass in New York. You can find anything in New York. The bluegrass that pushed its way up through the proverbial sidewalks and sprouted along the expressways of the five boroughs tended not to have south-ern-style mellowness or introspection, however. (Well, maybe there *are* some things you can't find in New York. . . .)

Just as it had in the land of the bean and the cod, although to a lesser extent, the folk boom boosted bluegrass in the Big Apple. Memorable bluegrass jam sessions became a regular part of the Washington Square Park folk music gatherings. Meanwhile John Herald, a livewire guitarist/vocalist frequenting the nearby Greenwich Village section of the city, was forming the Green-briar Boys with banjo picker Bob Yellin. They would have two talented mandolin players (Paul Prestopino, later a backup mu-sician for Peter, Paul and Mary and the Mitchell Trio; and Eric Weissberg, the future banjo king of the New York studio musi-cians, who played on the soundtrack of *Deliverance*) before recording with a third (Ralph Rinzler, the folklorist who would go on to help revitalize Bill Monroe's career, discover Doc Wat-son, and establish the Smithsonian's folklife program).

David Grisman, who would go on to become a major figure in the "new acoustic" music, helped found a bluegrass band called the New York Ramblers. They went the whole route: slowing down records from 33 1/3 to 16 rpm to decipher esoteric licks, buying string ties (found at a 42nd Street men's store), strapping the bass to the roof of a car and driving down to the Union Grove Fiddlers Convention to compete in the band contest—and win, as the Greenbriar Boys had before them.

Grisman's revolutionary musical tendencies should have been clear from such early instrumental compositions as "New York Ramble" and "Opus 54." What was clear was that the Yankees had arrived and were ready to burn a musical path through the bluegrass. This was no Shermanesque war of conquest; Bill Mon-roe himself drew on the talents of Yankees Bill Keith (in 1963) and Peter Rowan, Richard Greene, and Lamar Grier (1965–66) and reached a new creative peak in his career.

If it was war, it was a very civil one. An army of hot-picking long-haired Yankees would soon win the respect and sometimes the admiration of the bemused but unbowed southerners. And the monuments to the campaigns of the boys in blue bluegrass are still with us on records, tapes, and CDs.

Banjo Dan and the Mid-Nite Plowboys. *Banjo Dan and the Mid-Nite Plowboys,* Greener Pastures 003

Beacon Hill Billies. *Duffield Station,* East Side Digital 80652

Berkshire Mountain Boys. *Just for Tonite,* Acoustic Spinning Wheel 101

Bluegrass Supply Company. *Any Old Stretch of Blacktop,* Ma's 0055

Charles River Valley Boys. *Bluegrass Get Together with Tex Logan,* Prestige Folklore 14204

—————. *Beatle Country,* Electra 74006

Crooked Stovepipe. *Newfoundland Bluegrass,* Crooked Enterprises 8631

Gibson Brothers Bluegrass Band. *Underneath a Harvest Moon,* Bug Elm 4194

John Herald and the Greenbriar Boys. *The Best of John Herald and the Greenbriar Boys,* Vanguard 79317

David Grisman. *Earl Dawg,* Sugar Hill 3713 (includes the New York Ramblers)

Bill Keith and Jim Rooney. *Bluegrass: Livin' on the Mountain,* Prestige Folklore 14002

Kennebec Valley Boys. *Pride of Maine,* NQD 606

Buddy Merriam and Back Roads. *Mystery Train,* Lily Pad 529

Lee Moore. *Favorites,* Rural Rhythm 202

Northern Lights. *Take You to the Sky,* Flying Fish 533

—————. *Can't Buy Your Way,* Flying Fish 70593

Fred Pike and Sam Tidwell. *Flat Pickin' Something Different,* NQD 1808

Arnie Solomon. *Brooklyn to Galax,* Heritage C-642

Southern Rail. *Roadwork,* Turquoise 5083

—————. *Carolina Lightning,* Turquoise 5090

Tasty Licks. *Tasty Licks,* Rounder 0106

Joe Val and the New England Bluegrass Boys. *Bound to Ride,* Rounder 0109

Various artists. *Woodstock Mountains,* Rounder 3018 (Keith, Herald, Rooney, Happy and Artie Traum, and many others)

California There They Went: The Dillards, the White Brothers, and the West Coast Sound

> You can get the vibes you get when you're playing bluegrass, that feeling that happens at the moment and people vicariously get off on that feeling . . . It's a feeling goes deep, really deep within—it's like the *Call Of The Wild* when the dog stared into the fire.
>
> —Rodney Dillard to the author

It was pretty much like this. The Dillards, natives of Salem, Missouri, in the Ozark Mountains, decided to try their luck in the big city. But instead of going to Nashville or Washington, they packed up a station wagon and drove to Los Angeles. You could tell these boys were ready to think big and take a few risks. (Their baggage included a bass player who was so green on his instrument that he essentially learned how to play during the two-thousand-mile drive.)

The band: Rodney and Doug Dillard, Dean Webb, and Mitch Jayne were able to land a gig at an L.A. club. Fortune favors the bold, and in true Hollywood fashion an agent was in the audience one night looking for performers to play some thoroughly inbred hillbillies on a TV sitcom. The Dillards were signed up and soon became nationally famous as "The Darling Family" on *The Andy Griffith Show*. Doug was widely admired among aspiring pickers for being perhaps the fastest, cleanest, and brightest-sounding banjo player in captivity. Well, near captivity; Doug eventually left to pursue a career of let's-have-fun music while younger brother Rodney, iconoclastic but utterly serious about his art, led the band on to produce some of the most elaborate and adventurous bluegrass. At their best (and particularly in collaboration with Doug's initial replacement, Herb Pederson), the Dillards achieved a blend of hill-and-hollow deep feeling and horizon-wide musical expression that has never been equaled.

Eventually, the Dillards added drums, toured with pop star Elton John, and were generally accused by bluegrass traditionalists of ruining Western Civilization As We Know It. Ironically, Doug and Rodney had grown up in the very same primitive

mountain culture their suburban critics were idealizing and de-
fending; their witty storytelling bass player/front man Mitch
Jayne was a loving preserver of Ozark folkways. In addition, the
Dillards and Oklahoma native Byron Berline had collaborated on
one of the first all-fiddle albums featuring bluegrass backing, a
production released with scholarly notes by folklorist Ralph Rinzler that clearly documented the music's traditional roots.

Byron was the son of Lue Berline, a leading exponent of Texas
"contest" fiddling (so named because it was forged in the cru-
cible of fiddle contests that required lively but ultra-disciplined
performances of a spectrum of fiddle music used to accompany
different styles of dancing). He joined the Blue Grass Boys in
1967 and recorded the popular instrumental "Gold Rush."

He eventually made California his home base, forming the
Country Gazette band with a fellow Oklahoman, banjoist Alan
Munde. The Gazette for a time sought its fortunes more actively
on the bluegrass circuit of the South and the East Coast. Its sound
was less rock-oriented than the final evolution of the Dillards but
still highly adventurous, allowing the Country Gazette to have
years of success with traditional and newgrass audiences. (The
Gazette eventually made Texas its base state.)

The Dillards by no means first brought bluegrass to California
any more than Columbus first brought people to the Americas.
Several other transplants were making a go of their music in L.A.
If you liked the banjo picking on the soundtrack of the *Beverly
Hillbillies* television show, you were enjoying the picking of ex-
patriate southerner Don Parmley. (Yes, Flatt and Scruggs played
the theme song, but Parmley did most of the episode banjo.)
Parmley later formed and still leads the Bluegrass Cardinals, one
of the first of a new wave of "contemporary" bluegrass.

A mainstay of the California Sound were the White Brothers
(guitarist Clarence and mandolinist Roland), who formed the
nucleus of the Kentucky Colonels, a band that has achieved near
cult status in bluegrass. There are Japanese bluegrass fans who
listen almost exclusively to the White Brothers; they even have a
fan magazine devoted to the careers of Clarence and Roland.

If you think these bluegrassers might get mixed up with the
California folk-rock/country-rock scene, you're absolutely right.

14. Front Range (photo by Eric Webber).

And if you think the musical products of those heady (in more ways than one) days are worth hearing, right again.

Berline hooked up with Chris Hillman, bass player for the Byrds rock band, in a bluegrassy collaboration called the Flying Burrito Brothers. (That wasn't the only time Byron fiddled while rockers burned it: He's the fiddler you hear doing "Country Honk" with the Rolling Stones on *Let It Bleed*.) Hillman was a serious mandolinist who had had a band with Parmley and the Gosdin Brothers, the aptly named Hillmen. Meanwhile, Clarence White became a Byrd during that group's switch from psychedelia to country-rock. (Byrds founding member Roger—originally Jim—McGuinn was a banjo picker before he started soaring in L.A.)

White returned to bluegrass to play lead guitar in Muleskinner, a supergroup of hot young pickers assembled to share a California television special with Bill Monroe and His Blue Grass Boys. Along with Clarence were Monroe admirer David Grisman (mandolin) and former Blue Grass Boys Peter Rowan (guitar and lead vocals), Bill Keith (banjo), and Richard Greene (fiddle). What Muleskinner didn't know was that Monroe's bus would break down, forcing them to do the entire show. They more than rose to the occasion.

One of the best assemblages of talent to come out of California of late is the band of the same name. California features Byron Berline, Dan Crary, John Hickman, Steve Spurgin, and John Moore.

One household name in rock music—and a talent forever associated with the San Francisco music scene—is Jerry Garcia of the Grateful Dead. If you're presently unfamiliar with bluegrass and/or don't follow the Dead (I know there are a few of you out there, so before we go any further may I also regretfully inform you that Dwight D. Eisenhower is no longer president), you may be surprised to learn that Garcia was a serious banjo picker long before his famous psychedelic and country-rock ensemble achieved its present musical immortality. (It may seem odd to call anything Dead immortal, but that's accurate.)

Garcia was an aspiring bluegrasser in the early 1960s, when he began a long friendship with mandolinist David Grisman.

Garcia and Grisman would haunt Sunset Park in Jennersville, Pennsylvania, one of the country music venues where Yankee cognoscenti went to seek out the high lonesome sound long before it was fashionable to do so. Garcia soon relocated to San Francisco and became famous as the Dead's lead singer/songwriter/guitarist. (He also earned the sobriquet Captain Trips for his mastery of certain mental excursions.) But Garcia truly loved bluegrass. And he still does. He recently confessed that despite the long, strange, happy trip (and trips) of being in The Dead, his secret desire is to be a Blue Grass Boy.

In 1973, he did the next best thing. He joined with Grisman, Rowan, fiddler Vassar Clements, and bassist John Kahn as Old and in the Way, eventually recording an album of live and lively bluegrass, made all the more enjoyable by the palpable work Garcia had done to get his banjo chops together. Recently Garcia and Grisman have joined in other well-received bluegrass-flavored acoustic projects.

Here's a true story that, I hope, will prove to the skeptics that Jerry Garcia's dedication to bluegrass is quite genuine.

The summer prior to recording their live album, Old and in the Way appeared at a festival in Warrenton, Virginia. The promoter had advertised heavily on Washington-area FM stations that this was going to be a weekend of Peace, Love, Blues, and Bluegrass. Not surprisingly, he got a big cadre of rock-oriented first-time festival goers in addition to the seasoned bluegrass audience.

When O&ITW was announced with Garcia as a member, the Deadheads gasped in joyous surprise and flowed like the Youngstown flash flood to the front of the audience. I know, because I was already sitting there. I was soon surrounded by Garcia lovers requesting—loudly and quite insistently—their favorite Dead songs. O & ITW kept doing its show, but looked pretty uncomfortable knowing that the audience's focus had shifted completely off bluegrass and onto their friend with the banjo.

Finally a guy right behind me yelled plaintively, "But *Jerry!* We wanna hear *you!*"

Garcia smiled, bent down to his microphone, and replied, "(Expletive) you."

15. California (photo by Irene Young).

The guy behind me laughed. The crowd laughed. Best of all, they shut up and started listening.

That incident to me was also a microcosm of what happens whenever someone/something popular makes a bluegrass connection. Whether it's Jerry Garcia, movies like *Deliverance* or *Bonnie and Clyde*, television shows like *The Beverly Hillbillies* or *Andy Griffith/Mayberry RFD*, some die-hard traditionalists grumble about cheap commercialism. Meanwhile, a small but healthy percentage of the mass market invariably develops a serious interest in the music. They end up with a bunch of Flatt and Scruggs and Bill Monroe recordings on their shelves and banjos in their living rooms. And as the Bossman himself might say, that's a fine, that's a wonderful thing.

San Francisco, home of the Dead, has long been blessed with great bluegrass of a surprisingly traditional orientation. High Country, led by mandolin picker Butch Waller, has been producing high-quality material for nearly a quarter century (scary, isn't it?). As will be detailed in the chapter on women in bluegrass, such Bay-area bands as the Phantoms of the Opry, the Good Ol' Persons, and Grant Street have contributed much to the music. One musician who did stints in High Country and other Bay bands was the late Rich Wilbur, a singer/songwriter/guitarist of great inventiveness who regrettably died of liver failure in 1992. If you enjoyed the yodeling comedy number "She Slid Down the Mountain (On Her Little Old Lady Who)" as sung by Bette Midler in the movie *Big Business,* you were hearing Wilbur's work.

It's fascinating that bands as trail-breaking as the Dillards and as tradition-affirming as High Country were just a freeway ride away from each other in the days when the so-called California sound was ripening. The moral? Maybe there is no one West Coast bluegrass sound any more than there's a single variety of California wine.

But it's fair to say that West Coast bluegrass tends to be more folksy than country, more of the Smoky Mountains than of smoke-filled bars. Yet it's often as long on vista as the Pacific Coast Highway and as large in spirit as big sky country. This is especially true of the progressive Rocky Mountain bluegrass bands: They may not be as wildly adventurous as many of their East Coast peers, but they stay fresh and lively while some East Coasters get fried and frenzied.

Colorado has been home to two of the most popular bluegrass bands of recent years. Hot Rize featured Peter "Dr. Banjo" Wernick (he's got a Ph.D. in sociology, you see), the Country Cooking alumnus; lead guitar powerhouse Charles Sawtelle; singer/songwriter and mandolin/fiddle whiz Tim O'Brien; and inventive bassist Nick Forster. The group was actually two bands in one: Hot Rize, a progressive bluegrass ensemble, and the alter-ego group, Red Knuckles and the Trailblazers, a hilarious sendup of cowboy and western-swing ensembles. More recently, Front Range has been cooking and serving its music, which is particularly rich in exquisite original material, to earn a prime spot on the national bluegrass menu.

The Bluegrass Patriots, also of Colorado, are a less well-known but also well-regarded, creative band. Like Front Range, they feature a number of their own compositions. Meanwhile, nearby Montana has produced the Turtle Creek and Wheel Hoss bands. Foxfire is from Oregon, Loose Ties from Wyoming, and all have used the southern sound as a creative wellspring.

Perhaps the ultimate western bluegrass (geographically anyway) is found in Alaska. Carl "Buddy" Hoffman of the Pine Hill Ramblers made Alaska the setting of his groundbreaking bluegrass mini-opera *Red and Rusty*. He later relocated there from New Jersey and shows no signs of returning. More recently, Hobo Jim has been recording for a major folk music label backed by members of the New Grass Revival. And when Fairbanks holds its annual folkfest, the high lonesome sound is well represented.

Tundragrass? Well, why not?

Bluegrass Album Band. *Volume 3,* **Rounder 0180 (features the California connection)**

Bluegrass Patriots. *When You and I Were Young, Maggie,* **Red Feather 017**

California. *Traveler,* **Sugar Hill 3803**

Country Gazette. *A Traitor in Our Midst,* United Artists 5596

————. *Keep On Pushing,* Flying Fish 70561

————. *Hello Operator . . . This Is the Country Gazette,* Flying Fish 70112

Doug Dillard. *Heartbreak Hotel,* Flying Fish 447

Rodney Dillard. *Let the Rough Side Drag,* Flying Fish 537

The Dillards. *There Is a Time,* Vanguard 131/2

———— with Byron Berline. *Pickin' and Fiddlin',* Elektra 7285

Due West. *Due West,* Musix 103

Foxfire. *Starting Today,* Pinecone 1023

Front Range. *The New Frontier,* Sugar Hill 3801

————. *Back to Red River,* Sugar Hill 3811

The Good Ol' Persons. *Part of a Story,* Kaleidoscope F260

High Country. *Sunset on the Prairie,* Turquoise 5071

The Hillmen. *The Hillmen,* Sugar Hill 3719

Hobo Jim. *Where Legends Are Born,* Flying Fish 70520

Hot Rize. *Hot Rize,* Flying Fish 206

————. *Take It Home,* Sugar Hill 3784

Kentucky Colonels. *1965–1966,* Rounder 0070

————. *Appalachian Swing,* SS-31

————. *Long Journey Home,* Vanguard 77004

Loose Ties. *Up and Down the Highway,* Snake River 012

Muleskinner. *Muleskinner Live,* Sierra 6001

————. *A Potpourri of Bluegrass Jam,* SX-6009 (newgrassy studio album)

Old and in the Way. *Old and in the Way,* Sugar Hill 3746

The Pine Hill Ramblers. *Red and Rusty,* Revonah 911

Traditional Ties. *Traditional Ties,* Sugar Hill 3748

Turtle Creek. *Busy Signals,* Turtle Creek 0001 [Neb/Mont]

Various artists. *Highlights of the '91 Fairbanks Summer Folk Fest,* Real Time [no number]

Wheel Hoss. *Northern Plains,* Cowboy Heaven 0003

Rich Wilbur. *In the City,* Sophronie 545

ELEVEN

GLORYLAND

Bluegrass Gospel

I do not see any reason why the devil should have all the good
tunes.
—Rowland Hill, English preacher and hymn publisher

Here's a mystery: How does bluegrass religious music manage
to appeal to people from a spectrum of religious and philosoph-
ical backgrounds? How can it be that bluegrass gospel songs—
largely derived from fundamentalist Protestant traditions—are
heard and even sung with joy by Catholics, Jews, and agnostics?

These questions have importance because if you listen to
bluegrass, you're going to hear songs about Jesus and heaven.
Sunday mornings at bluegrass festivals are typically devoted to
"sacred songs" and no major bluegrass band has failed to record
in this genre. Even if you believe in neither Christ nor Gloryland,
I expect you're going to find something lovely and meaningful
in gospel music.

Part of bluegrass gospel's appeal is its ability to be glowingly
beautiful one moment and bursting with sheer exuberance the
next. How could you not be moved by that? You don't need
to be a Christian to be enthralled by Bach's "Jesu, Joy of Man's
Desiring" or Handel's *Messiah*. Those classical classics are so

magnificent that they transcend faiths, thus paradoxically allowing the faiths that inspired them to shine through.

But it's also interesting to note that the Protestantism that inspired southern sacred music was of an independent variety,
steadfast in its beliefs but less tied to organization, doctrine, and
dogma. A popular gospel composition sums it up: "You go to
your church and I'll go to mine/But let's walk along together."
(For a perceptive exposition of this phenomenon, see "The Old
Time Element: Religion and Fiddle Music," chapter 8 of Neil V.
Rosenberg's *Bluegrass: A History.*)

The Methodists, Baptists, and Presbyterians of the South were
certainly religious fundamentalists. The Methodists in particular
were a revivalist sect known for emotional "camp meeting"
gatherings. This type of worship, which in its extreme form
could involve ecstasies, falling to the ground, and/or speaking
in tongues, was termed "pentecostal" or "holiness" by its adher-
ents and "holy rolling" by its detractors. Even today, old-timers
refer to uplifting, "testifying" gospel music as "holiness
singing."

It is crucial to understand that the holiness sects were also non-
formalistic and nonhierarchical, stressing a direct relation of the
individual with God. There was an emphasis on other-worldli-
ness, on seeking revelation and salvation. This outlook survives
in bluegrass gospel in such songs as "This World Is Not My
Home" and "Farther Along."

Mountain Protestantism lent bluegrass gospel not only phi-
losophy but musical technique. The influence of church harmonies on Bill Monroe and his peers has already been noted. Another survival in bluegrass of rural church singing is the practice
of "lining the hymn," a type of responsive singing where the
minister would sing a line that would then be sung back by the
congregation. This pattern repeated itself for a total of seven
lines, each sung by the minister and echoed in the response, con-
cluding with an eighth and final line sung in unison. This style
owes much to the camp-meeting and "holiness" tradition; it was
also extremely practical in the days when hymnals were scarce
and literacy rates low.

Southern audiences constituted a ready market for gospel music, and performers were happy to oblige. It is significant to note that of the sixty sides recorded by the Monroe Brothers during their career, twenty-eight—nearly half—were hymns or religious songs. Indeed, their first big-selling record was "What Would You Give in Exchange for Your Soul?"

Rural revivalism did much more than shape the material of southern white gospel music. Religious "camp meetings" were destined to have a broader influence. Understand that audiences sat in the open air facing not a small pulpit but a stage; on this stage were held a variety of preaching and musical activities. Those gathered brought food and enjoyed "singing all day and dinner on the ground" (a practice later immortalized in a gospel song made famous in bluegrass by Jimmy Martin), and the faith-

16. The Lewis Family (courtesy of Stan and Sylvia Wilkinson, Delmar Studios).

ful could socialize with their neighbors in a manner that would not be possible within a church building. This format probably influenced the structure of later country music parks and bluegrass festivals with their stages and structured activities alongside the overall informality and family picnicking.

Among the leading exponents of the holiness style of singing has been the Sullivan Family of Alabama, descendants of J. B. Sullivan, a logger who played old-time fiddle and banjo. His son Arthur had a spiritual experience in 1939 after a nearly fatal illness and turned full time to the ministry. He also sang and was joined by his brother Jerry and his son Enoch. The trio accompanied themselves on mandolin, guitar, and fiddle. With the addition to the band in 1949 of Margie Brewster Sullivan, Enoch's wife, the group became a beloved regional attraction. It has gained additional popularity through exposure on the bluegrass festival circuit. Over the years, the Sullivans have attracted such talented sidemen as Joe Stuart and Marty Stuart.

Doyle Lawson and his band Quicksilver have been making an increased number of appearances at all-gospel shows, featuring a mix of uptempo vocals backed by driving instrumental work and a cappella selections. Unaccompanied singing, often in a responsive mode, has its roots in the deep mountain congregations too small and poor to afford pianos or organs. It is not uncommon in bluegrass; Ralph Stanley in particular has done stunning a cappella work. But the unaccompanied harmonizing of Quicksilver, the Nashville Bluegrass Band, and others seems to owe more to African-American song stylings than to traditional white hymn singing. It is an exciting new trend in bluegrass.

The Sullivans, Quicksilver, the Marshall Family, and bluegrass veteran Carl Story are a few of the acts closely identified with bluegrass gospel. But it is the Lewis Family of Georgia that truly makes "a joyful noise" and is called "The First Family of Bluegrass Gospel" (a self-description, yes, but also totally undisputed).

The Lewis Family has taken exuberant holiness singing to another energy level. Most classic bluegrass bands have used sparse instrumentation behind their gospel quartets (eg., Monroe—mandolin, guitar, occasional bass; Flatt and Scruggs—fingerpicked guitar by Earl, occasional rhythm guitar by Lester, bass). The Lewis Family puts a full band sound replete with driving banjo phrases and tambourine-banging rhythm behind their soaring harmonies. Add to that a fast-paced, highly professional stage show spiced by the antics of "Little Roy" Lewis, one of the most energetic comedians on any stage today, and you have quite a show.

This show got its start in 1951 when the family was asked by the Woodmen of the World club to do a program of gospel music at its supper in Thomson, Georgia. The core ensemble of Elsey, Talmadge,and Wallace had been performing as a string band called the Lewis Brothers, but with the addition of Pop Lewis (Roy, Sr.) and sisters Polly and Miggie, the band took off. (Janis, another sibling, later joined the band to create a powerful three-sister vocal section.) And true to scripture, a little child did lead them: Little Roy Lewis, then a precocious 9-year-old.

The Lewis Family was greatly influenced by such artists as The Chuckwagon Gang (the quintessential mixed-voice country mini-chorus), the Masters family, Martha Carson, and Bill Monroe. Little Roy claims that the first gospel record he ever heard was Monroe's "Shine, Hallelujah, Shine," purchased when the family didn't even have a record player and the disc had to be taken to a neighbor's house to be heard.

Little Roy can be one of the most lovably outrageous performers ever to take over a stage. In the words of an autobiographical roof-raising song, he's "a crowd pleasin' man." The family has obviously heard his routines more than once over four decades of performing. Yet at each show they seem to be in a very genuine state of bemusement, wondering just what he's going to say or do next.

This popping picker with the broad grin is a superb musician whose sharply punctuated guitar and banjo work is essential to the Lewis sound. Driven by a rolling rhythm section and topped by a powerhouse vocal lineup, the camp-meeting, revival-style Lewis sound never falters from the first tambourine tap to the last banjo crescendo. Despite some personnel changes over the years, the band has shown great consistency. The Lewis Family is also a successful little cottage industry. (The 38-year run of their Augusta, Georgia, television show must have set some kind of national programming record.)

Pop Lewis typically ends each performance by stepping to the mike and asking the audience, "Have you enjoyed the Lewis Family?" The invariable increase in applause makes the answer clear.

An even greater compliment, I think, is this: My friends in the progressive band Bottle Hill were an aggregation of such varied tastes that they argued constantly over which bands were best. With one exception.

You guessed it. Everybody, but everybody, loves the Lewis Family. Just as everyone—even if secretly—treasures expressions of the triumphs and yearnings of the soul.

Paul Adkins and the Borderline Band. *Wings of Gold,* **Rebel 1676**

Bluegrass Cardinals. *What Have You Done for Him,* **Bluegrass Cardinals 1004**

Bluegrass Meditations. *Walking in the Light of His Love,* **Rich-R-Tone C8117**

Gary Brewer and the Kentucky Ramblers. *Nearing Jordan's Crossing,* **CC-0122**

Chestnut Grove Quartet. *This Old World Is Full of Trouble,* **C-5914 (a cappella)**

Country Gentlemen. *One Wide River to Cross,* **Rebel 1497**

The Cox Family and Alison Krauss. *I Know Who Holds Tomorrow,* **Rounder 0307**

J. D. Crowe and the New South. *The Model Church,* **Rebel 1585**
———. *Calling My Children Home,* **Rebel 1574**

East Ohio Grass. *Sing Gospel by Request,* **Gloryland GLP 1492**

Forbes Family. *Gleams of That Golden Morning,* **Rebel 1631**

Furman Boyce and the Harmony Express. *Through Heaven's Door,* **Atteiram 1674**

Gillis Brothers. *Sunshine in the Shadows,* **Hay Holler Harvest 303**

Randall Hylton. *Slippers with Wings,* **Old Homestead 70088**

Jim and Jesse and the Virginia Boys. *I'm Gonna Sing, Sing, Sing,* **Double J Entertainment 1006**

Doyle Lawson and Quicksilver. *I Heard the Angels Singing,* **Sugar Hill 3774**

————. *Treasures Money Can't Buy,* **Brentwood 5303**

Lewis Family. *Sweet Dixie Home,* **CDO-2849**

————. *Live in Georgia,* **RS-2861**

————. *Golden Gospel Best,* **Holly 254**

Lost and Found. *Hymn Time,* **Rebel 1668**

Claire Lynch. *Friends for a Lifetime,* **Brentwood 5362**

Marshall Family. *The Best of the Marshall Family,* **Rebel 1652**

Bill Monroe and His Blue Grass Boys. *Cryin' Holy,* **MCA 10017**

Charlie Moore and Bill Napier. *Country Hymnal,* **King 917**

New Tradition. *Seeds of Love,* **Brentwood 5231-J**

The Pitneys. *Higher Places,* **Harvest 1206**

Reno and Smiley. *16 Greatest Gospel Hits,* **HCD 125**

The Rising Wind. *Gospel,* **Heartland 520**

Sacred Sounds of Grass. *Eternal Highway,* **LC 38019 (German bluegrass gospel band singing in English)**

Seldom Scene. *Baptizing,* **Rebel 1573**

Ralph Stanley. *Back to the Cross,* **FRC-638**

————. *Almost Home,* **Rebel 1707 (a capella gospel)**

The Stanley Brothers and the Clinch Mountain Boys. *Hymns And Sacred Songs,* **King 645**

————. *Old Country Church,* **Holly 127**

Carl Story and the Rambling Mountaineers. *Bluegrass Gospel Collection,* **CMH 9005**

The Sullivan Family. *Bluegrass Gospel,* **Loyal 168**

Jerry and Tammy Sullivan. *A Joyful Noise,* **Country Music Foundation 016**

Traditional Grass. *I Believe in the Old Time Way,* **Rebel 1708**

Rhonda Vincent and the Sally Mountain Show. *Bound for Gloryland,* **Rebel 1692**

Doc Watson. *On Praying Ground,* **Sugar Hill 3779**

TWELVE

THE WOMEN

Seen and Definitely Heard

The rooster crows, but the hen delivers.
                    —motto of the Dixie Chicks band

Yes, bluegrass vocals have been defined by high male harmonies, and the macho instrumentals owe more than a little to male hormones. But women have long been part of the music, as witness the careers of Sally Forrester, Ola Belle Campbell, Gloria Belle, and Rose Maddox. And there's no question that the most talked about bluegrass star of the 1990s has been Alison Krauss.

It's fair to say that female artists have had a higher profile plus greater success and longevity in country music than in rock-n-roll, where female rockers only began significantly coming into their own in the late 1970s. In fact, country music star Patsy Montana is believed to be the first woman in pop music history to have a million-selling hit with "I Want to be a Cowboy's Sweetheart."

Many female country singers whose careers were launched from the 1940s through the 1960s have influenced the styles of women in bluegrass, so just a few of them should be mentioned here. LaVerne Williamson Davis, a Kentucky native who became nationally famous under her professional name of Molly O'Day, was a traditionally-oriented performer who popularized a belt-it-out style. Kitty Wells, the "Queen of Country Music" on WSM's Opry, evinced more of a country elegance. Patsy Cline, also considered one of the immortals of country music, could produce a mournfulness that was heartrending yet beautifully understated. More recently, Loretta Lynn and June Carter Cash have been highly successful with lovely but gutsy deliveries owing much to their Appalachian roots.

Occasionally, women in country music encountered traditional country values. In the early 1940s, Roy Acuff hired a banjo-playing comedienne named Rachel Veach for his band. He called her Cousin Rachel, but this was not enough for many fans, who felt it improper for a single female to be touring with a band. Acuff, not wishing to fire her, took to introducing dobro player Beecher "Pete" Kirby as "her great big bashful brother Oswald." Fans were satisfied that Ms. Veach was properly chaperoned, and Kirby was ever after known professionally as Brother Oswald.

Bill Monroe featured Sally Forrester (wife of his fiddler Howdy Forrester; no chaperone problem there) in the Blue Grass Boys of the early 1940s, and her accordion playing marked an interesting experimental phase in a music that was eventually to again become and remain a string-band music.

Jimmy Martin also featured "girl singer" and guitarist Lois Johnson in concert as far back as 1960. Later, Gloria Belle was a featured Sunny Mountain Boy (person?) and she remains one of the best female bluegrass lead vocalists ever. Belle owes a debt to the Molly O'Day school of singing, as do Wilma Lee Cooper, Rose Maddox, and other female country singers who have had some association with bluegrass.

But why were women not a part of bluegrass from the start? Maybe for the same reason that women have only recently made strides in rock-n-roll: the lingering notion that a female can't perform a tough, uncompromising music "like a man." (Funny how people who claim this forget blues or soul vocalists like Bessie Smith, Janis Joplin, and Tina Turner. . . .)

Or maybe it has something to do with males bonding into bluegrass bands and women not even trying to fit in. Those days are gone forever as women open every door in the arts. But there's an important non-sexist musical hurdle that sometimes keeps men and women from making beautiful bluegrass together.

Bluegrass is truly the high lonesome sound and it thrived, as Bill Monroe discovered, when the high ranges of the male voice were exploited. As mentioned earlier, Johnny Cash could record a version of "Roll in My Sweet Baby's Arms" in his trademark gravelly baritone, which would be nice but wouldn't have that bluegrass edge to it. (And as also mentioned earlier, the performances of amateur bands playing and singing that classic in the key of G are suddenly transformed when they are encouraged to pitch it up to B-flat or even B.)

On the face of it, it would seem that a woman singing high harmony above two men in a bluegrass trio would be a great addition to any band. And that's often the case, giving female vocalists their long overdue value as members of bluegrass ensembles. But what is a high singing range for a man is often a low range for most women. Therefore the harmony lines can be correct but that "edge" isn't always there.

There are several solutions to this, and their use has gone together with the increased success of women in bluegrass. One solution is simply all-women bands in which the vocal ranges meld the best. Another is using two female voices as the predominant sound in a trio, with a third (high) male voice added at the bottom of the harmony. Or there's the Osborne Brothers approach: Keep the high lead singing on top with no harmonies over it in the chorus; instead, stack other voices under the lead.

A real breakthrough came in the early 1970s, when a pioneering band called Buffalo Gals made a strong showing on the bluegrass festival circuit. In the late 1970s, Katie Laur was fronting a band (of men) to audience acclaim in Cincinnati, Washington, and other serious bluegrass towns. Today, the New Coon Creek Girls, Wildwood Girls, All Girl Boys, and other bands have enthusiastic followings who are tuned into their music. "Girl pickers" are no longer gimmicks. Murphy Henry not only picks the banjo but is actively involved in producing teaching videos.

17. Laurie Lewis (photo by Irene Young).

If there was a barrier to women in bluegrass that made them a lingering curiosity, it may have continued through doubts that any female could be the boss of a successful full-time professional band. Those doubts have evaporated like mountain dew in a summer sun with the successes of Laurie Lewis with her Grant Street Band and, in particular, Alison Krauss, leader of Union Station and a true superstar within today's bluegrass world.

Laurie Lewis is a California native, born into a family of flutists, pianists, and hymn singers. (Her father had been a wind player in the Dallas Symphony.) After family moves to Texas and Michigan, Lewis ended up back in San Francisco with its burgeoning bluegrass scene. She learned fiddle playing and repair, too, running her own violin shop in San Rafael for six years.

One of her first major band experiences came as bass player with the popular Bay-area group, Phantoms of the Opry. But she kept up on the fiddle, soon winning state championships. Lewis was a founder of The Good Ol' Persons (love these band names!) and a member of Blue Rose, something of a female folk-bluegrass supergroup whose lineup of popular performers included banjoist Cathy Fink, guitarist Marcy Marxer, dobroist Sally Van Meter, and bassist Molly Mason.

It is with her band Grant Street that Laurie Lewis has achieved her recent success as singer, instrumentalist, and songwriter. Her clear folky voice, so well suited for ballads, is also capable of powerful country yodeling (a talent Lewis says she got not so much from classic Jimmie Rodgers or Bill Monroe recordings as from practicing a Tarzan yell when she was a kid). The coed talent of Grant Street has included Tony Furtado, now one of the country's top newgrass-style banjo players.

Alison Krauss was born in Illinois to parents who loved music from folk songs to show tunes. She took up the fiddle as a child and entered her first contest at age nine, placing fourth in the twelve-and-unders. Krauss was soon fiddling—and singing—with country and bluegrass bands.

While Krauss was a member of Classified Grass, she sang lead on a demo tape that came to the attention of Rounder Records. The company offered her a chance to record an album and appear at the Newport Folk Festival. Within a few years she was becoming hugely popular, touring with her band Union Station. The questions about "Can a woman play bluegrass?" subsided, only to be replaced with rounds of questions about "How can you be so young and lead a band?" (Krauss was born in 1971.)

Meanwhile, her career was highlighted by exclamation points: Krauss won rave responses from audiences both within and well outside the traditional bluegrass world, top honors from the major bluegrass music associations, Grammy nominations, and awards. A major breakthrough came when Krauss and Union Station were awarded membership on the roster of the Grand Ole Opry, the first bluegrass act to be so honored in decades.

As a vocalist, Alison Krauss—in quality, sensitivity, and power—has been called something of a bluegrass Dolly Parton. While this is an apt comparison, Krauss lists her early singing influences as Ricky Skaggs and Tony Rice, and currently admires Ralph Stanley, Larry Sparks, the Cox Family, with whom she has recorded a gospel album, and Rhonda Vincent. She's sure to be an influence on others in the years to come. With the advent of Alison Krauss, a major bluegrass career has been launched.

Like Grant Street, Union Station has showcased the talents of an important new banjo talent. Alison Brown is a native Californian but her bluegrass influences were more "southern" than Laurie Lewis's—that is, Los Angeles instead of San Francisco. Brown was tied into the L.A. music scene when the Dillards and the team of Berline, Crary, and Hickman were active there. Later she headed east and gained national exposure with the progressive Massachusetts band Northern Lights while attending Harvard Business School. But Brown became disenchanted with the unreasonable eighty-hour-a-week demands of an investment banking career, became a full-time musician (talk about giving up your day job!) and is today one of the most popular new banjo pickers around, male or female.

Rhonda Vincent is another fiddler with exceptional singing abilities. Vincent, who also plays a crisp mandolin, has been praised by critics and held in high esteem by no less a colleague than Alison Krauss.

The Good Ol' Persons is still active and has featured the

18. Alison Krauss (photo by Alan Messer).

talents of Kathy Kallick, a guitarist who has proven herself an expressive singer/songwriter, and double-talent dobroist/lead
singer Sally Van Meter, both of whom have recorded solo albums. Another major female bluegrass performer who has made
her mark as a singer, banjo player, and band leader is Lynn Morris.

Bluegrass, as has been noted, is historically an outgrowth of
country music and also a style of modern folk music with traditional roots. Folksingers Joan Baez and Dian used the Greenbriar
Boys as a backup band on notable occasions in the early 1960s.
Today's female bluegrass vocalists often evince a strong-edged
country-and-western flavor to their singing. But there are many
exceptions, even among singers well known in Nashville.

Country-rock star Emmy Lou Harris achieves a highly successful blend of sweetness and strength in her interpretations.
This Alabama native started out as a folksinger in the Joan Baez
and Judy Collins mode and was also greatly influenced by folk-
rock legend Gram Parsons. From 1975 to early 1990, Harris
achieved huge success with her blend of rock and country music. Her backup group, the aptly named Hot Band, was fronted
for a time by Ricky Skaggs. But Harris was no stranger to bluegrass, having guested with the Seldom Scene. She decided to get
into the music seriously and formed an equally hot acoustic
group called the Nash Ramblers (featuring guitarist Randy Stewart, mandolinist/fiddler Sam Bush, and banjo picker Al Perkins).

Sharon and Cheryl White were brought into the business by
their father Buck (a Texas native whose multiple skills on mandolin and piano owe much to the twin influences of bluegrass
and western swing) and his wife Pat. Originally known as the
Down Home Folks, the Nashville-based Whites' band helped
bring the sweet-singing sisters to prominence just as attitudes toward women in bluegrass were changing.

Ginger Boatwright, formerly of Red, White and Bluegrass and
the Doug Dillard Band, is associated with the Nashville bluegrass scene but sings with an unornamented, almost Appalachian directness, even when assaying contemporary material. Indeed, the hills that gave birth to bluegrass still exert their
power over the music. The Carter Family, featuring sisters-in-

law Sara and Maybelle, greatly influenced the sounds that finally became bluegrass. Hazel Dickens of West Virginia, who frequently performs with Alice Gerrard, is well on her way to becoming one of the living legends of mountain music. Dickens' intense mountain-bred voice is often raised in song about coal miners' struggles or the lot of women in modern society. (Her composition "You'll Get No More of Me," also recorded by Lynn Morris, comes close to being a bluegrass feminist anthem.)

It is little known that James Monroe was not the only child of the Father of Bluegrass to go into music: Bill's daughter Melissa Monroe recorded several bluegrass singles for Columbia Records in 1950 and 1951. Unfortunately, they have not been reissued as of this writing and Miss Monroe died in 1990 at the age of 54. But she still lives on in her poignant composition, "Is The Blue Moon Still Shining?" which has been recorded by her father and other artists.

The All Girl Boys. *Heart's Desire,* **Wilder Shore 101**

Linda Barker and Appalachian Trail. *I Could Cry,* **Heartland 518**

Nancy Blake. *Grand Junction,* **Rounder 0231**

Ginger Boatwright. *Fertile Ground,* **Flying Fish 70550**

Louisa Branscomb. *It's Time to Write a Song,* **Lodestar 004**

Alison Brown. *Twilight Motel,* **Vanguard 79465**

Julie Ann Carpenter. *Fiddlin' Up a Storm,* **Redbird NQD-8816**

Sara and Maybelle Carter. *Sara and Maybelle Carter,* **Bear Family 15471**

Kathy Chiavola Band. *Labor of Love,* **My Label KCP-1001**

Wilma Lee Cooper. *Wilma Lee Cooper,* **Rounder 0143**

Hazel Dickens, *Hard Hitting Songs for Hard Hit People,* **Rounder 0216**

———. *Matewan,* **Daring 1011 (soundtrack of John Sayles film)**

Dixie Chicks. *Thank Heavens for Dale Evans,* **Dixie Chicks Records 1**

Cathy Fink. *The Leading Role,* **Rounder 0223**

Emmy Lou Harris and the Nash Ramblers. *At the Ryman,* Reprise 9-26664-2

Murphy Henry. *M&M Blues,* Arrandem 80

Kathy Kallick. *Matters of the Heart,* Sugar Hill 3820

Alison Krauss and Union Station. *Two Highways,* Rounder 0265

————. *I've Got That Old Feeling,* Rounder 0275

————. *Everytime You Say Goodbye,* Rounder 0285

Laurie Lewis and Grant Street. *Singin' My Troubles Away,* Flying Fish 515

————. *True Stories,* Rounder 0300

Laurie Lewis and Kathy Kallick. *Together,* Kaleidoscope 44

Rose Maddox. *Rose Maddox Sings Bluegrass,* Capitol 1799 (with uncredited guest appearances by Don Reno on banjo and Bill Monroe on mandolin)

————. *The One Rose,* HAT-3056

Lynn Morris Band. *Lynn Morris Band,* Rounder 0276

————. *The Bramble and the Rose,* Rounder 0288

New Coon Creek Girls. *So I'll Ride,* Turquoise 5075

————. *The L&N Don't Stop Here Anymore,* Pinecastle 1027

Molly O'Day. *In Memory,* Old Homestead 196

Petticoat Junction. *Lonely Old Depot,* Pinecastle 1017

Sidesaddle. *Daylight Train,* Turquoise 5080

Karen Spence and the Friends of Bluegrass. *With Love to Daddy,* Webco 0116

Sally Van Meter. *All in Good Time,* Sugar Hill 3792

Rhonda Vincent. *Timeless and True Love,* Rebel 1697

————. *A Dream Come True,* Rebel 1682

The Whites. *Forever You,* MCA 960

THIRTEEN

ACROSS THE BORDERS
AND THE DEEP
BLUE SEAS

A true friend is one soul in two bodies.

—Aristotle

Looking back on it, a major event occurred on a Saturday after-noon in June 1970, when a young band called the Bluegrass 45 took the stage at Bill Monroe's festival in Bean Blossom, Indiana, and turned out to be one of the hits of the show. The guys said they took their band name from the year 1945, when Monroe had his first recording sessions with Earl Scruggs on banjo and de-fined the bluegrass sound we know today.

But 1945 was significant for another reason: It was the year a lot of the men in that Bean Blossom audience had stopped fight-ing the fathers and uncles of the boys in this band. The Bluegrass 45, you see, was from Japan.

Audiences chuckled quietly at the band's English. The Blue-grass 45 cleverly played on this, producing a wild version of the Stanley Brothers "Still Trying to Get to Little Rock." Renamed "Still Trying to Get to Bean Blossom," the exchanges between the

19. Kazuhiro Inaba (photo by Wayne Dunford).

"farmer" and the lost "stranger" were all in Japanese, with just enough English words and phrases popping up now and then to make the whole thing hilarious. But the crowd applauded loudly and was on its feet at the band's versions of the instrumental classics "Dueling Banjos" and "Foggy Mountain Breakdown."

Of course, southerners have also chuckled at Yankees trying to sing country music and African-American musicians have been amused by white boys trying to sing the blues. But instrumental work—good ol' pickin'—is a universal language, and many downhome musicians have suddenly realized that the newcomers actually have something to teach them on the instrumental side.

20. Kukuruza (photo by Jim McGuire).

Overseas bluegrassers are now experiencing the same challenge faced by Yankees in the 1950s and '60s: how to learn the music pretty much at second hand, through recordings and rare local appearances by touring stars. And they too are responding magnificently. Old-time-style mountain music produced in Japan, Britain, and other countries has grown from a curiosity into a fully developed art form. Bluegrass is doing the same. It's not just for collectors anymore, although unfortunately you may have to make a little extra effort to find it.

Whereas British, European, and Japanese musicians used to pretty much produce derivative versions of bluegrass (and in heavily accented singing voices at that), the best of overseas bluegrass is now a further dimension of the genre. Japanese pickers are turning out highly original instrumental recordings. They are particularly strong in capturing the spirit of old-time string band music, with some recordings by Japanese banjo/fiddle ensembles having the same heart and spirit as an old 78 rpm disc of hillbilly, but without the scratches.

The Land of the Rising Sun smiles on bluegrass, and major American stars enjoy triumphant concert tours there. The nation continues to make its own contributions to the genre with characteristic Japanese inventiveness. (At the risk of purveying national stereotypes, I would venture to suggest that a people that over the years has immediately understood and adopted western imports from the locomotive to baseball to consumer electronics would immediately latch onto the beauties and intricacies of the banjo.)

Josh Otsuka, mandolin player of the Bluegrass 45, returned to America to become a highly regarded member of the Washington, D.C., bluegrass scene. More recently, Kazuhiro Inaba has emerged as a highly regarded Japanese banjo and guitar picker; Hikaru Hasegawa is a leading exponent of Japanese newgrass; the Tiger Cats perform bluegrass rock; and there are even Japanese women's bluegrass bands (one fittingly calling itself Today).

Bluegrass is beloved not only in Japan but also in Canada, Britain, Europe (including Russia), Australia, and New Zealand. (It probably tinkles away in somebody's Walkman at an Antarctic research station too.) Perhaps the most exciting thing about all this is that international bluegrass is not a pale, pathetic recycling of the American version. Local musicians are melding their folk music traditions with the idiom, creating new variations.

For example, Andrew Roblin, a Canadian now performing full time out of Pennsylvania, has been consciously using the sounds of his native Manitoba to create his own brand of bluegrass. He recommends this approach to bluegrassers everywhere so that, as much as we love those hills of old Virginia, we don't have to slavishly sing about them, especially if we didn't come from there. Veteran radio performer Tom Wilson deserves mention here for his genial song stylings and keen ear for great but underappreciated material by Gordon Lightfoot and other fellow Canadians.

21. Beppe Gambetta (photo by Stefano Goldberg).

In regard to the rest of the overseas English-speaking world, it should be noted that for years the British have been fiercely dedicated interpreters and historians of America's rural string band traditions. Australia has produced some great musicians and was also the land of John Edwards, whose peerless study of the music was cut short by his death in a car accident.

European pickers have been highly successful at adding their own folk traditions to bluegrass while building on the work of American newgrassers. A few of the most talked about are Slavek Hanzlik, a Czechoslovakian guitarist and mandolinist now living in Canada; Italian newgrass guitarist Beppe Gambetta; and Kukuruza, a Russian bluegrass band that has landed an American recording contract and artistic representation.

What about the singing? One myth about foreign bluegrass is that the picking may be good but the accents ruin it. Not true. Often the English is perfectly fine. Remember, these artists have been listening to our records over and over (and anyway, foreigners are often fluent in English while we self-satisfied Americans struggle shamefully with a few words of another language). Even in the worst cases, the English probably won't sound any stranger to you than a Yankee twang does to a southerner.

I won't pretend to have heard all the artists listed below, but the ones I haven't heard have received appreciative reviews in the bluegrass press (country of origin and any additional information included in parentheses). And I've found this to be true: If a band has the persistence to make a recording and then get their product over here, they're probably real good. The hassles of doing all that constitute a mighty powerful selection process.

Beutling Brothers. *Turn the Green Grass Blue,* **Wonderland Records 9003 (Germany)**

Bluegrass Breakdown. *Light Up the Night,* **Undo 49 503 CY (Germany)**

Bluegrass Connection. *The Path of Least Resistance,* **Bluegrass Connection 102 (Canada)**

Bluegrass 45. *Caravan,* **Rebel 1507 (Japan)**

Beppe Gambetta. *Dialogs,* Brambus 199122-2 (Italy)

———— with Tony Trischka. *Alone and Together,* Brambus 199124-2

Goldrush. *Crossing the Blue Ridge,* Nugget 93001 (Scotland)

Gone at Last. *Gone at Last,* Big Hand 14009 (Norway)

Grassoline. *Mother Nature's Door,* Strictly Country 22 (Holland)

Groundspeed. *Charlotte's Waltz,* Elite Special 733 507 (Switzerland)

Slavek Hanzlik. *Spring in the Old Country,* Flying Fish 79582 (with Americans Bela Fleck, Stuart Duncan, and Mark Schatz)

————. *Summer Solstice,* MUSA MCD 93-2

Hikaru Hasegawa. *Show by Banjo,* Rolling Hills 0002 (Japanese newgrass)

Kazuhiro Inaba. *Hard Times, Come Again No More,* Red Clay 109 (Japan)

————. *Goin' Across the Sea,* Hay Holler Harvest 104 (with guest appearances by Bobby Hicks, Butch Robbins, Don Stover, and Herschel Sizemore)

Svata Kotas. *Pozde V Noci/Neskoro V Noci (Late at Night),* G-Music 001 (Czechoslovakian banjo player; Tony Trischka– and David Grisman–influenced newgrass)

Robert Krestan and Second Grass. *Revival,* Monitor 01 0039 –2 331 (Czechoslovakian mix of Monroe bluegrass, folk, and rock)

Kukuruza. *Crossing Borders,* Sugar Hill 3814 (Russia)

Emory Lester. *The Emory Lester Set,* Northumberland Records 025 (Grismanesque new acoustic music from Canada)

Orchard Sessions 93. *A Canadian Bluegrass Sampler,* BGC-103 (Canada)

Quartet. *Stranka Pametoi,* Duna [no number] (Czechoslovakia)

Rank Strangers. *Kamara,* T.O.R. 002 (Australia)

Red Wine. *Full Taste,* Red Wine 002 (Italian band featuring Beppe Gambetta)

Andrew Roblin. *Andrew Roblin, John Lionarons and the Pocono Mountain Boys*, Upstart 1002 (Canadian influence)

Sieker Band. *Appaloosa*, LP Records LC 8276 (Germany)

Station. *Lonesome Train*, Playasound 65072 (France)

De Stroatklinkers. *Vlaigende Grunneger*, SK 101 (Holland; folky sound with some vocals in Dutch)

Tiger Cats. *Race Is On*, Rolling Hills 0001 (Japanese bluegrass rock)

Today. *Little Girl's Heart* [no label] (Japanese female bluegrassers)

Various artists. *Bluegrass '90*, Panton 81 0972–4311 (Czechoslovakian bands)

————. *Galax International*, Heritage 067 (broadranging collection of competitors from Australia, Japan, Britain, and other European nations at the annual old-time, mountain, and bluegrass music contest in Virginia)

————. *Long Journey Home*, International Bluegrass Music Association [no number] (International)

Tom Wilson. *Electric Radio*, Rodeo 8010 (Canada)

FOURTEEN

THREE WAYS TO TOMORROW

Newgrass, Country 'Grass, and the New Traditionalism

Every man's got a right to his own style.

—Bill Monroe to the author

Newgrass and New Acoustic Music

It was a small but pivotal moment. New York City banjo picker Roger Sprung played a track by New England banjo picker Bill Keith off his *Living on the Mountain* album for upstate New York banjo picker Tony Trischka.

It was 1964 and the selection featured Keith's break to "Salty Dog Blues," a fun but familiar G-E minor-A-D progression that Keith had suddenly charged up five quantum energy levels with his innovative straight-melody-line picking. Instead of grabbing a fistful of chords with his left hand and running the standard right-hand three-finger, Scruggs-style blender through them, Keith was off on a musical steeplechase of a melody line running all over the neck of his banjo. "Every banjo player's jaw dropped to the floor back then when they heard that," Trischka recalled years later.

It was not only a revelation for Trischka but an intersection among three musicians who would influence not only the banjo but the development of what is now famous (and to some, infamous) as "newgrass music."

Roger Sprung was one of the first New Yorkers to master Scruggs-style banjo. He emerged from the bluegrass jams at the now legendary Washington Square Park folk sings and then became notorious as an exponent of what he termed "progressive bluegrass." In this musical idiom, nothing was out of bounds: sea chanties, baroque classics, Broadway hits, Sousa marches, and Jewish dance melodies in addition to bluegrass standards and Scots-Irish fiddle tunes were all given the special Sprung twist. In more ways than one: Roger is probably the only banjo player in the world to have Keith-style tuners on all five strings of his instrument. And he uses them, too. Sprung's recordings from the 1960s with instrumental whizzes Jon Sholle (guitar) and Jody Stecher (mandolin) showed other musicians of the day that it was possible to keep pushing the envelope. (Today, Sprung's musical partner is Hal Wylie, a fine interpreter of British ballads.)

Bill Keith's influence as a developer of the melodic style of banjo playing was immense. Concurrent with southerner Bobby Thompson, Keith developed a method of using a three-finger picking style combined with deft fretting work that allowed straight melody lines. This was a major departure from Scruggs-style, in which there is only one melody note for every three or four accompanying rhythm/fill notes in a picking pattern. (For more, see the chapters on Monroe and on early Yankee bluegrass plus the appendix section on the banjo.) "Keith-style banjo" facilitated the playing of fiddle tunes note for note—and a whole lot more.

All manner of jazzy variations were now possible. Add on chromatic scales and augmented chords and a strange and wonderful new world opened up. Trischka was one who entered deeply.

A softspoken musical rebel from Syracuse, New York, he became a mainstay of the newgrass bands Country Cooking and Breakfast Special, and later formed his own group, Skyline.

Among the collective alumni of these three bands: Pete Wernick on banjo; Kenny Kosek on fiddle; Lou Martin (aka Tersh Gilmore), Andy Statman, and Barry Mitterhoff on mandolin; Russ Barenberg and John Miller on guitar; Stacy Phillips (aka Mel Marshall and Moshe Savitsky) on dobro; Roger Mason and Larry Cohn on bass; and vocalists Nondi Leonard, Jim Tolles, Danny Weiss, and Dede Weyland. Most continue to be active on the music scene.

The metro New York newgrassers didn't start out to offend anyone anymore than Picasso did when he painted two eyes on one side of a face. They just loved music and artistic challenges and their attitude was, "Hey, let's try this!"

Meanwhile, mandolinist David Grisman had left the New

22. New Grass Revival: John Cowan, Bela Fleck, Pat Flynn, Sam Bush (courtesy of Bluegrass Unlimited).

York/New Jersey metro area for California, where he became a
major player in the "new acoustic" music, which developed in
parallel with newgrass. Grisman was influenced by bluegrass
mandolinists Bill Monroe and Frank Wakefield, French violinist
Stephane Grapelli, and Grapelli's Belgian gypsy partner, the legendary guitarist Django Reinhardt. Grisman was joined by mandolinist Mike Marshall, violinist Darol Anger, and even bluegrass flatpicker Tony Rice in perfecting a jaunty, syncopated
style that took full advantage of the woody sound of unampli-
fied instruments. (Reinhardt was long dead, but Grisman and his
collaborators soon realized several collaborations with the still-
vital Grapelli.)

This new acoustic music has little significant relation to the
ethereal romanticism of "new age" music. It is similar to newgrass except that it has been more heavily influenced by jazz and
does not look to the banjo as its main voice.

Bluegrass traditionalists reacted with some ire to the jazzy minor sixth and suspended chords and the rock accents being
played by the newgrassers, especially when the perpetrators
started getting invitations to major festivals. Let's face it: an album entitled *A Robot Plane Flies Over Arkansas* (Tony Trischka at
the controls) is bound to be considered musically and even po-
litically suspect. But newgrass was never a plot, a challenge, or a
conscious heresy. It just evolved under the big city influences of
rock, jazz, Latin salsa, Jewish klezmer, and the international
sounds now widely referred to as "world music."

In fact, the broadranging interests of newgrassers often
worked against them. So eclectic were they that they sometimes
didn't develop a "sound" that would appeal to a cohesive audience. Bands such as Breakfast Special developed enthusiastic
cult followings but never broke through to wide appeal. Only recently have the musical enthusiasms of audiences broadened
enough to match the tastes of the performers.

But Tony Trischka had appeal as a solo artist, perhaps because
the banjo was something to focus on. His adventurous, sharply
accented, and ultimately logical flights of musical fancy directly
inspired such formidable talents as Tony Furtado and Bela Fleck,
who took the 5-string to astonishing fusion explo-implosions

with his band the Flecktones. (Meanwhile, Trischka has become the ultimate traditionalist by championing the banjo music of the West Africans and the early minstrels.)

New Yorkers were not the sole creators of newgrass. California, as we've seen, has had its share of artists sounding the beautiful wooden grains of their instruments against the prevailing grains of accepted form. And a band from Louisville was so significant it gave the new music its name.

That band was the New Grass Revival, an outfit with a make-new-fans-while-taking-no-prisoners approach (example: their show-stopping arrangement of "Great Balls of Fire"). The initial Revival foursome were Curtis Burch, guitar and occasional dobro; Courtney Johnson, banjo; Ebo Walker, bass; and Sam Bush, mandolin and fiddle. Bush epitomized the band: hardwired talent, long hair, and a 110 percent energy level at every concert ("pickling fast," as the liner notes to their first album described it). He had recorded with banjoist Allen Munde as part of Poor Richards Almanac, considered another of the pioneering newgrass ensembles. When a teenager, Bush won a prestigious fiddle contest but refused to wear the regulation western shirt and little string tie when it came time to have his picture taken for the contest's Hall of Fame. Thus the hall had a blank picture frame for that year, and Bush was proud of sticking to his principles.

Like the Dillards and their Elton John tour, the Revival was a huge success when it traveled with Leon Russell (who later recorded "Roll in My Sweet Baby's Arms" for one of his albums). This method of bringing bluegrass new recognition did not sit well with traditionalists, of course. But to young rock audiences grooving on the Allman Brothers and the Grateful Dead, the Revival represented this stuff called bluegrass that they had heard was pretty cool. And they loved it. To their peers—and to listeners today—the New Grass Revival created some of the flat-out best music ever to issue from banjos, mandolins, guitars, and basses.

Certainly some of the most original music ever to issue from anyone has been the gift of an old friend of the Dillards and the Revival, John Hartford. Yes, the same musician who composed the lovely "Gentle on My Mind," which has become one of the most recorded songs in history. Hartford is truly one of a kind. He's like a lanky reincarnation of Uncle Dave Macon. He writes nutty songs, he is a licensed riverboat pilot in his spare time, and although he isn't really newgrass in the jazzed out, rocked out sense, he has to go somewhere so you'll be sure to listen to him. Soooo. . . .

Today some observers feel that newgrass is in decline due to the rise of the new traditionalism. As of this writing there aren't New Grass Revival- or Skyline-style bands on the scene. Coming close is the Sugarbeat ensemble headed up by Tony Furtado. But individuals—usually banjo pickers—still employ newgrassy approaches in their music: Andy Owens, Dennis Cyporyn and Scott Vestal.

Some newgrassers still fear that their smallest deviations from three-chord bluegrass will be condemned as crass commercialism no matter how empty their bank accounts are, and some tra-

23. David Grisman and Jerry Garcia (photo by Susan Millman).

ditionalists dread that true bluegrass will be poisoned by electric instruments and weird chords. Both sides may wish to ponder a greater possibility—the growth of another grassy style.

Right now the ultimate demonic offspring from matings of rock with old-time music and bluegrass are Bad Livers and Killbilly. Bad Livers, which performs such delectations as "Chainsaw Therapy" and "Clawhammer Fish," has been described as punk old-timey. Killbilly has been described as "pedal-to-the-metal bluegrass from hell." (I prefer to think of them as The Red Hot Chili Peppers Eat the Stony Mountain Boys and Not the Other Way Around.) It's pretty amazing stuff.

And what you should know is that alternative rock audiences *love* Bad Livers and Killbilly. This may be the future. Don't ask me if it works.

Bad Livers. *Horses in the Mines,* **Quarterstick 20**

The Big Dogs, with Tony Trischka. *Live at the Birchmere,* **Strictly Country 24 (Harley Allen, Red's son; David Grier; fiddler Andrea Zonn; and bassist Debby Nims)**

Country Cooking. *Barrel of Fun,* **Rounder 0033**

Dennis Cyporyn. *I Must Be Dreaming,* **Krypton KR0014**

Bela Fleck. *Inroads,* **Rounder 0219**

————. *Drive,* **Rounder 0255**

Tony Furtado. *Sugarbeat,* **Planet Bluegrass 2001**

Jerry Garcia and David Grisman. *Jerry Garcia/David Grisman,* **Acoustic Disc 2**

David Grisman. *The Rounder Album,* **Rounder 0069 (combination of bluegrass and new acoustic)**

Tom Hanway. *Bucket of Bees,* **Joyous Gard [no number]**

John Hartford. *A John Hartford Anthology,* **Flying Fish 440**

————. *Nobody Knows What You Do,* **Flying Fish 028**

John Hartford and Mark Howard. *Cadillac Rag,* **Small Dog A-Barkin' SD-191**

Kilbilly. *Foggy Mountain Anarchy,* **CCR-9451-2**

Bill Knopf. *Pacific Swing,* **FIR-001**

Livewire. *Wired!,* **Rounder 0281 (with Scott Vestal, banjo)**

Lou Martin. *Recent Work,* Rounder 0214 (aka Harry Gilmore of Country Cooking, with C. C. alumni Tony Trischka and Russ Barenburg)

James McKinney. *Mind Over Banjo,* McKinney C-11-9

New Grass Revival. *New Grass Revival,* Hollywood 307 (re-release of explosive Starday debut album)

————. *Anthology,* EMI 94624

————. *Fly Through the Country,* Flying Fish 032

————. *Too Late to Turn Back Now,* Flying Fish 050 (live at the Telluride Festival)

Andy Owens Project. *Kerosene Circuit,* Real Records 2001

Peter Rowan. *Medicine Trail,* Flying Fish 071

Roger Sprung and His Progressive Bluegrassers. *Roger Sprung and His Progressive Bluegrassers,* Verve/Folkways 9037

Tony Trischka. *Bluegrass Light,* Rounder 0048 (includes several tracks with the Breakfast Special band lineup)

————. *A Robot Plane Flies Over Arkansas,* Rounder 0171

————. *World Turning,* Rounder 0294 (an anthology of banjo music from West-African roots through old-timey, ragtime, and bluegrass to punkgrass)

Tony Trischka and Skyline. *Skyline Drive,* Flying Fish 388

————. *Fire of Grace,* Flying Fish 479

Country 'Grass

As traditional as the music is, unless it grows it starts dying.
—Ricky Skaggs, during an appearance on The
Nashville Network

Just a few years ago, if a popular young bluegrass performer had gone off to Nashville to make his fortune playing country music, there would have been much wailing and lamenting and gnashing of teeth and rending of garments among the bluegrass faithful.

"Why have you forsaken us?" would be among the more polite (and printable) comments. Having been steeped in tales of

how old-fashioned country music sold out to rhinestone-
and electric-guitar commercialism, dyed-in-the-true-blue bluegrassers get pretty tetchy if they think it's happening again.

So how do we explain the affection felt by bluegrassers for
Ricky Skaggs, Marty Stuart, and the late Keith Whitley? These
performers cut their teeth, tuned their vocal chords, and lim-
bered their picking fingers on bluegrass. Skaggs and Whitley
spent their high school vacations touring with Ralph Stanley.
Stuart was a boy-wonder mandolin player playing with Lester
Flatt. (When asked where he grew up, he replies truthfully, "In
the back of Lester Flatt's bus.") Then all three go off to Nashville
and become some of the biggest stars of the "new country"

24. Lou Reid, Terry Baucom, and Carolina (courtesy of Lou Reid, Terry Baucom,
and Carolina).

boom. Yet no one in bluegrass hates them, which again proves how popular they are.

The answer has to do with Skaggs, Stuart, and Whitley themselves and with what the new country music is all about. It also has to do with a new style of bluegrass that is variously called contemporary or country 'grass.

These three musicians were immensely talented and genuinely likable, and Whitley's death was a terrible loss. What's appreciated by bluegrass fans is that Skaggs and Stuart haven't forgotten their roots and seem ready to pick and preach bluegrass at any opportunity. As Skaggs proclaims in one bluegrass-flavored country hit, "I'm just a country boy, country boy at heart." The music video for this chart climber depicts Skaggs as a Manhattan executive who receives a surprise visit from a rural relative, his Uncle Pen, who looks around Skaggs' fashionable midtown office and says, "I heard it was bad, boy, but I never thought you'd sink to this." "Well," says Skaggs rather meekly, "this is pretty good. . . ." Of course, after picking and singing his way across Times Square and through the subway, Skaggs convinces his crusty relation that he really is still a country boy. What makes this little film especially funny is that Uncle Pen is played by none other than Bill Monroe.

The new Nashville looks kindly on Monroe and on bluegrass in general. This is a happy surprise. Once country music got glittery, it seemed embarrassed by its roots and looked on bluegrass as a poor cousin, in much the same way the soul music industry didn't have much time for the old blues. What's more, today's country-and-western industry is so youth-oriented that many beloved older stars (such as Merle Haggard and George Jones) can't get much air play for their music, despite having loyal followings. The difference seems to be that today's country music stars and audiences have grown up loving folk music and bluegrass. Acoustic music seems awesome, not old-fashioned. And of course, they're right.

Meanwhile, a goodly portion of today's bluegrass audience has grown up listening to slick country-and-western music. Its tempos, themes, and instruments don't seem foreign or particularly threatening. So when a young bluegrass group sings about truck drivers instead of train engineers or honky-tonks instead of the lonesome pines, when the band has a little more of a boom-chucka country-and-western beat and less of a bluegrass surge in its timing, when the bass is electric, it's not as great a departure as it used to seem.

The reader may notice that I have just slipped in an operational definition of what contemporary "country 'grass" is. If the above paragraph doesn't exactly define country 'grass, it sure helps identify it. (Incidentally, a lot of people drop the "blue" and call it grass, a contraction that further identifies this music as being basically bluegrass, though different from the original stuff.)

Unlike next-door neighbors who cut their lawns to different lengths, there's not always an immediately noticeable dividing line between country 'grass bands and the new traditionalists (see below). Obviously some bands with an electric bass will play a straight-up Stanley Brothers song in mournful mountain style while a straight-arrow bluegrass band will launch into a Hank Williams honky-tonk number. Some bands, like the immensely popular Alison Krauss and Union Station, play hardcore bluegrass one moment and country-flavored ballads the next. It's interesting to note that three musicians who gained prominence during their membership in Union Station—guitarist Tom Stafford, mandolinist Adam Steffy, and bassist Barry Bales—were all graduates of the bluegrass program at East Tennessee State University, which may soon be to bluegrass what the University of Southern California film school is to the cinema.

But something is happening and it goes back a few years. Jim and Jesse, the Osborne Brothers, and even Jimmy Martin were known for their country-and-western-flavored bluegrass. The Bluegrass Cardinals, who were hailed in the 1970s as proof that someone besides the newgrassers could produce exciting young bands, were in some ways harbingers of the uptown 'grass that was to come. Two Cardinals alumni, guitarist David Parmley (Don's son) and mandolinist Larry Stephenson, have successfully continued that trend in recent solo albums. (In Stephenson's case, an apparent Osborne influence helps make the grass/country circle complete.)

25. Rising Wind (photo by Louie Kesterson).

Ricky Skaggs' star rose with several solo albums, a fiddling stint with the Country Gentlemen, and membership in Emmy Lou Harris's Hot Band. His major contribution to country 'grass was in the formation of Boone Creek with Jerry Douglas (dobro), Wes Golding (guitar), and Terry Baucom (banjo), who all became big names in the modern country and bluegrass scene. Tim O'Brien, formerly with Hot Rize, has been playing well-turned country and swing with a flavor close to bluegrass.

John McEuen, a driving force behind the Nitty Gritty Dirt Band's historic musical summit with traditional-style country veterans, *Will the Circle Be Unbroken,* has recently assembled dream bands for his aptly-named String Wizards projects. In this vein, the East Coast's answer to the band California may be

26. IIIrd Tyme Out (courtesy of Ray Deaton).

Chesapeake, composed of veterans Mike Auldridge, T. Michael Coleman, Jimmy Gaudreau, and Moondi Klein. A group of formidable professionals who usually appear in backup roles in other bands now frequently perform together at the Station Inn, a popular Nashville bluegrass destination, under the appropriate name the Sidemen. Other country 'grass groups spawned by the Nashville scene include the New Kentucky Colonels, the Cluster Pluckers, and the Bluegrass Idles.

Mark O'Connor, who conquered all comers in the Texas fiddle contest wars and later appeared in the country-jazz-rock instrumental fusion band the Dregs, has joined with dobro whiz Douglas in the house band of The Nashville Network's popular *American Music Store*. Both O'Connor and Douglas are reckoned

27. The Lonesome River Band (courtesy of Acoustigrass Entertainment).

by many to be the finest all-around performers on their instruments today.

And there's guitarist Peter Rowan, who under the tutelage of Monroe blossomed into a compelling singer equally capable of infectious joy and soul-rending plaintiveness. Rowan is one of the most enjoyable and truly original talents on the American music scene, and is so multi-talented and eclectic that he defies categorization. (I've solved the problem by mentioning him in both the country 'grass and new traditionalist categories. I wish I could do the same with all the overlapping talents on today's bluegrass scene.)

The Rising Wind features impressive original material penned by the band's members. Lou Reid, Terry Baucom and Carolina, the Lonesome River Band, Paul Adkins and the Borderline Band, IIIrd Tyme Out, the Bass Mountain Boys, Special Delivery, and the Virginia Squires are considered country 'grass by some and firmly "in the tradition" by others. If there's a secret to their success (besides having talent!) it may be this: Have good songwriters in the band and/or seek out the best new original material by up-and-coming songsmiths, but don't forget to add a few favorite old bluegrass standards to your repertoire.

To use a popular phrase, country 'grass seems to be a win-win situation.

Paul Adkins and the Borderline Band. *Modern Times,* **Rebel 1701**

————. *How Many Roads,* **Rebel 1711**

James Bailey. *Genesis II,* **Heritage 098**

Beaver Creek. *Having a Wonderful Time,* **Pinecastle 1019**

Bluegrass Cardinals. *New and Old Favorites,* **BGC 1002**

Boone Creek. *Boone Creek,* **Rounder 0081**

Chesapeake. *Rising Tide,* **Sugar Hill 3827**

Cox Family. *Everybody's Reaching Out for Someone,* **Rounder 0297**

Gary Ferguson. *Without You,* **Turquoise 5084**

Foxfire. *Starting Today,* **Pinecastle 1023**

Hazel River Band. *One Step Ahead,* **Hay Holler Harvest 401**

Jerusalem Ridge. *North Wind,* JR020591

John McEuen. *String Wizards,* Vanguard 79462 (including Sam Bush, Buck Graves, Stuart Duncan, Jerry Douglas, and David Grier)

————. *String Wizards II* (the above plus guests David Grisman, Darol Anger, Tony Rice, Byron Berline, Jose Feliciano, and others)

Lonesome River Band. *Carrying the Tradition,* Rebel 1690.

Tim O'Brien and the O'Boys. *Oh Boy! O'Boy,* Sugar Hill 3808

Mark O'Connor. *The New Nashville Cats,* Warner Brothers 26509

David Parmley. *Southern Heritage,* Rebel 1706

Radio Flyer. *Old Strings New Strings,* Turquoise 5079

Lou Reid, Terry Baucom, and Carolina. *Carolina Moon,* Rebel 1712

Reno Brothers. *Kentucky Gold,* Webco 0142 (Ronnie, Dale, and Don Wayne Reno)

————. *Acoustical Celebration,* Webco 0145

Larry Rice. *Time Machine,* Rebel 1656

————. *Artesia,* Rebel 1666

Rice Brothers. *Rice Brothers,* Rounder 0265

The Rising Wind. *Original,* Heartland 516

Rowan Brothers. *Tree on a Hill,* Sugar Hill 3823 (Peter, Christopher, and Lorin)

Peter Rowan. *Walls of Time,* Sugar Hill 3722

The Sidemen. *Almost Live at the Station Inn,* Red Clay 112

Ricky Skaggs. *That's It!,* Rebel 1550

————. *Sweet Temptation,* Sugar Hill 3706

Special Delivery. *This Is Special Delivery,* Pinecastle 1020

Larry Stephenson Band. *Wash My Blues Away,* Webco 0144

Stony Lonesome. *Blue Heartache,* Red House 51

IIIrd Tyme Out. *Puttin' New Roots Down,* Rebel 1703

————. *Grandpa's Mandolin,* Rebel 1713

Virginia Squires. *I'm Working My Way,* Rebel 1642

Wild and Blue. *Heirloom,* Pinecastle 1021

The New Traditionalism: Cutting a Full Circle in the Bluegrass

We listen with more pleasure to the hillbilly in proportion as
our urban life turns more and more into ferro-concrete.
                    —Jacques Barzun, American musicologist

My first experience of the Johnson Mountain Boys was frightening. I'm not kidding.

I had heard a lot about them, and as soon as they walked out
on stage at the Spirits of Bluegrass Festival and raised their instruments to the waiting mikes I could see they weren't just a
nostalgia trip in their suits, red string ties, and white Stetsons.

28. The Johnson Mountain Boys (photo by Dane Penland).

They were authentic. *So* authentic looking and sounding that I felt I had been swallowed by a time warp.

In a genuinely unnerving fantasy, I was no longer sitting on the grass and under the stars in the Mennonite country of Pennsylvania. I felt I had been transported back to 1954 and the Take-It-Easy Ranch in Maryland. Hearing the real stuff in a low-ceilinged room. Raw. Yet polished. Bluegrass before it was even called that. Not that I wouldn't like to go back to those thrilling days of yesteryear, but falling through time this way was like going over the highest hump on a roller coaster of particularly nasty height.

And like being on a roller coaster, the experience of seeing and hearing the Johnson Mountain Boys elicited whoops and adrenaline rushes. The fans of traditional bluegrass were ecstatic. Here was the true bluegrass (It's alive, alive!), not a stuffed museum piece. Here was real bluegrass with as much crack and sparkle as anything the newgrassers were putting out (So there!), but it was lonesome in the way only the Monroe/Stanley stuff can be.

The whole thing was summed up for me afterwards when I told Eddie Stubbs how much I liked his fiddle playing and how much it reminded me of Paul Warren, longtime Foggy Mountain Boy.

"Yes," said Stubbs in his bassy voice. (Gosh, I thought, he even *talks* a little like Paul Warren!) "I'm pretty much of the blood, thunder, and razor blades school of bluegrass fiddling."

The impact of the Johnson Mountain Boys cannot be overestimated (nor can the despair of traditionalists when for a brief period they disbanded). But in retrospect, the triumphal resurgence of traditional-style bluegrass should have come as no surprise.

The success of the 1971 three-record set *Will the Circle Be Unbroken* should have announced as clear as the guitar run into "Orange Blossom Special" that there was a huge audience for straight country music of the kind you used to get down on the farm before "the Nashville sound" came along, all slickly packaged and devoid of nutrients. The success—artistic and commercial—of this unprecedented collaboration of the Nitty Gritty Dirt Band with such country music veterans as Roy Acuff, Maybelle Carter, Jimmy Martin, Earl Scruggs, Merle Travis, and Doc Watson should have been a wakeup call. (Bill Monroe declined to participate in the *Circle* project. Contrary to popular assumption, it probably wasn't the long hair or funky name of his would-be musical hosts that turned him off. Monroe feels strongly that his Blue Grass Boys are an essential part of his sound and rarely records without them.)

In the mid-1970s, five young but well-seasoned bluegrass stars recorded a tribute to the music simply entitled *The Bluegrass Album.* The menu of this tasty record consisted of what might be termed the Not Overdone Greatest Hits of Bluegrass. The highly successful result (which has inspired several follow-up albums) was embraced by a "silent majority" of traditionalists who feared

29. The Bass Mountain Boys (photo by Mike Mayse Photography).

that the music would pass with its old gods to be replaced by the heresy of the demon newgrassers.

But its success was by no means guaranteed. Even the most dedicated traditionalists had to admit in private that there was no surfeit of bands recycling the old stuff. And the ones who were, of course, were not doing it as well as the originals, thus making modern "traditional" bluegrass an increasingly boring nostalgia trip. But the band had immense talent: J. D. Crowe (banjo), Tony Rice (guitar and lead vocals), Doyle Lawson (mandolin), Bobby Hicks (fiddle), and Todd Phillips (bass). Later, other equally great musicians would appear on the series including Jerry Douglas (dobro), Mark Schatz (bass), and Vassar Clements (fiddle). And they were playing the old straight stuff but in their own way, which made it both familiar and fresh. The Bluegrass Album Band, as it came to be known, was a harbinger of the resurgence of straight bluegrass and the potential of "superband" collaborations.

Mandolinist David Grisman took time off from defining his brand of new acoustic music to fill studios on a couple of occasions with traditional-style bluegrass greats. Banjo picker Larry Perkins is among many others who have taken the same approach recently.

Mainstream bluegrass shows no signs of drying up. In fact, there's been a flood of traditional-style. If popular tastes go in cycles, the lonesome pines of bluegrass are emerging from a dry spell and becoming true evergreens. Great lead singing, which was somewhat eclipsed by the clamor for hot instrumental work, is now regaining audience attention. The careers of Del McCoury and Peter Rowan have been boosted, and lesser known but still excellent vocalists like Dave Evans and Bob Paisley are gaining new fans. And the children of bluegrass artists are founding a new generation.

What the Bluegrass Album Band has done on occasion the Johnson Mountain Boys, the Bluegrass Band (featuring Butch Robbins on banjo), Lonesome Standard Time, Bill and Terry Smith, Special Consensus, the Traditional Grass, and the Nashville Bluegrass Band have done on a more regular basis. The Nashville Bluegrass Band has gone from strength to strength with excellent original material and a penchant for marvelously chilling a cappella gospel material. Although bluegrass obviously doesn't get the kind of airplay that the new country music enjoys, the fact that a traditionally-oriented bluegrass band was founded in Nashville says a lot for current attitudes towards a sound that the industry once largely ignored.

Outside Nashville there are bands bucking trends and defying categorization. Notable example: The Dry Branch Fire Squad, led by Ron Thomasson, wry mountain music philosopher and former Ralph Stanley sideman. Were Thomasson there beside you as you ponder this tome, he would doubtless urge you not to be messed up by musicology or flummoxed by folkloristics, but simply to remember that lonesome is a car up on blocks.

30. Glen Duncan, Larry Cordle, and Lonesome Standard Time (photo by Lance LeRoy).

Traditional-style bluegrass is going on and on, down through the years, and will land in the twenty-first century alive and sod-kicking. Around about 2039 A.D., when it celebrates its 100th birthday, we'll truly be able to drop the "style" qualifier and just say "traditional." The music will have deserved that.

It's fitting to note that when the Nitty Gritty Dirt Band got around to producing a second *Circle* album, its high point had to be "When I Get My Rewards." This stunning track featured the woody, lonesome mandolin and impassioned vocals of Levon Helm of The Band. Levon Helm, whose memory of having his brain tattooed as a child by the sights and sounds of the classic 1946 Bill Monroe and His Blue Grass Boys opened this book. So

31. Lost and Found (courtesy of Lost and Found).

let's come full circle with that circle around a music that keeps on rewarding us.

Appalachian Express. *Walking the Blues,* **Rebel 1684**
Bass Mountain Boys. *Carolina Callin' Me,* **Pinecastle 1001**
———— **with Chubby Wise.** *Fiddlin' with Tradition,* **BMM-0014**
The Bluegrass Album Band. *Volume One,* **Rounder 0140,**
————. *Volume Two,* **Rounder 0164**
————. *Volume Three,* **Rounder 0180**
————. *Volume Four,* **Rounder 0210**
————. *Volume Five,* **Rounder 0240**

32. The Nashville Bluegrass Band: Alan O'Bryant, Stuart Duncan, Gene Libbea, Roland White, and Pat Enright (photo by Jim McGuire).

The Bluegrass Band. *Second Cut,* Hay Holler Harvest 100 (featuring Butch Robbins, banjo)

Larry Cordle, Glen Duncan, and Lonesome Standard Time. *Larry Cordle, Glen Duncan and Lonesome Standard Time,* Sugar Hill 3802

Dry Branch Fire Squad. *Long Journey,* Rounder 0289

———. *Just for the Record,* Rounder 0306

Leroy Eyler and the Carroll County Ramblers. *Mysteries of Life,* DaBoDoLee 7-7-89

Dave Evans. *Classic Bluegrass,* Rebel 1119

———. *The Vetco Sessions,* Vetco 3033/6

Gillis Brothers. *Ice Cold Stone,* Hay Holler Harvest 302

David Grisman. *Home Is Where the Heart Is,* Rounder 0251/2 (with Red Allen, Del McCoury, and others)

Mitch Harrell. *Influences,* Pinecastle PRC 1012

Hazel River Band. *One Step Ahead,* Hay Holler Harvest 401

Johnson Mountain Boys. *Requests,* Rounder 0246

———. *At the Old School House,* Rounder 0265 (live show)

———. *Blue Diamond,* Rounder 0293

Lonesome Standard Time. *Mighty Lonesome,* Sugar Hill 3816

Lost and Found. *January Rain,* Rebel 1702

———. *Classic Bluegrass,* Rebel 1112

McPeak Brothers. *Makin' Tracks,* Rebel 1612

Nashville Bluegrass Band. *Waitin' for the Hard Times to Go,* Sugar Hill 3809

———. *The Boys Are Back in Town,* Sugar Hill 3778

The New Tradition. *Love Here Today,* Brentwood Music 5285J

Nitty Gritty Dirt Band. *Will the Circle Be Unbroken,* United Artists 9801

———. *Will the Circle Be Unbroken Two,* UVL 12500

Bob Paisley and the Southern Grass. *No Vacancy,* Brandywine 1002

Parmley and McCoury. *Families of Tradition,* BGC-1003

Larry Perkins. *A Touch of the Past,* Pinecastle 1022 (featuring guests Earl Scruggs, Mac Wiseman, the Osborne Brothers, Alison Krauss, John Hartford, Del McCoury, and others)

Lou Reid. *When It Rains,* Sugar Hill 3788

Lou Reid, Terry Baucom, and Carolina. *Carolina Blue,* Webco 0143

Peter Rowan. *The First Whippoorwill,* Sugar Hill 3749 (tribute to the music of his old boss Bill Monroe)

————. *All on a Rising Day,* Sugar Hill 3791 (with the Nashville Bluegrass Band)

Charlie Sizemore Band. *Back Home,* Rebel 1705

Bill and Terry Smith. *The Grass Section,* Red Clay 111

Bobby Smith and the Boys From Shiloh. *Across the Blue Ridge Mountains,* FF9591

Dallas Smith and the Boys from Shiloh. *Tribute to Bobby Smith,* Atteiram 1703 (with Bill Monroe, Glen Duncan, Buck Graves, John Hartford, Kenny Baker, and other guest artists)

South Central Bluegrass. *We Can't Return to the Homeplace,* Webco 0130

Special Consensus. *Green Rolling Hills,* Turquoise 5089

String Fever. *Save Your Heart,* Beaver 01

Traditional Grass. *Howdy Neighbor Howdy,* Rebel 1698

————. *10th Anniversary Collection,* Rebel 1718

Bluegrass Sponsors

Many bluegrass and old-time fans are dead-set against "commercialization." In fact, some self-appointed guardians of The Music rant and rave and rail and invoke the dreaded C-word the moment that music gets any national exposure.

True, pop culture tends to either roll over or co-opt traditional music and crafts. Yes, there is a cheapening, diluting, lowest-common-denominator effect when commercial interests seize upon a folk art and repackage it for mass consumption.

But bluegrass and old-time music were made possible by modern commercial radio and recordings—and by commercial sponsorship.

Along with picks, strings, instruments, and other tools of the trade (which musicians have endorsed as readily as athletes sign shoe contracts) a wide and wacky range of products and services have kept bread on the tables of blue-grass musicians and thereby kept bluegrass music in our ears.

The chart below is offered for your edification.

Sponsor	Product or Service	Beneficiary	Comments
Sears, Roebuck	department store	"National Barn Dance" program on WLS Radio, Chicago	The store owned the station. The call letters stood for "World's Largest Store."
Crazy Water Crystals Co.	natural mineral laxatives	The Monroe Bros., Tennessee Ramblers, the Tobacco Tags, and others on the WBT "Barn Dance" show, Charlotte, North Carolina	Sponsor was one of the first companies to use country music as a national ad medium (circa 1933).
Alka-Seltzer	indigestion relievers	WLS "National Barn Dance" program	When NBC picked up the show and broadcast it throughout the then-48 states, a full hour of each program was sponsored by that speedy fizz.
National Life and Accident Company	insurance	The "Grand Ole Opry" on WSM Radio, Nashville	The company owned the station. The call letters stood for "We Shelter Multitudes."
Man-O-Ree	laxatives	Charlie Monroe	Charlie owned the product, which was created and produced by a

Sponsor	Product or Service	Beneficiary	Comments
			small-town pharmacist and sold via mail order through his weekly radio show.
Jim Walter Corporation	prefab homes	The Stanley Brothers	At the time, Ralph and Carter were based in Live Oak, Florida, trying to survive the rock-n-roll avalanche.
Kroger Stores	supermarket chain	Don Reno and Red Smiley	Don and Red (who were also sponsored by a car dealer and a furniture store during their career) did a great TV show sponsored by Kroger. Highlight: The boys join the host in singing "Let's go Krogering, it's the only way to shop!"
Martha White Co.	flour and baking goods	Flatt and Scruggs, Jim and Jesse	Famous slogan: "Goodness Gracious, It's Good!" Famous ingredient: "Hot Rize" (that later inspired the name of a progressive bluegrass band). Fifteen Minutes of Media Fame: Theme song sung at fans' request during Flatt and Scruggs concert at Carnegie Hall.

Sponsor	Product or Service	Beneficiary	Comments
Goo Goo	candy bars	Various artists on the Grand Ole Opry	Jingle: "Go get a Goo Goo/ It's good!" Popular myth: That "goo" stands for "Grand Ole Opry" (the product predates the show).
Hoyt Sullivan	hair products, liniments and furniture polish	The Lewis Family gospel music TV show, which ran for 38 years on WJBF, Augusta, Georgia	"By His blessing they multiply greatly." —Psalm 107:38
Coburn Furniture Co.	furniture	"	"
Dr. Victor Castella	optometry	"	"
Kennedy's Mixture	ulcer medicine	"	"
Thomas Homes	builder	"	"
Martha White	baking products	"	"
Mac's Trailer Sales	trailers	Bill Harrell on WSVA, Harrisonburg, Virginia	The sponsor became upset when Harrell let a snuff-dipping little old lady sing on his show and demanded auditions for future guests. On this basis, Harrell asked an unknown (to him) band, the Statler Bros., to audition. They didn't call back. The next Harrell heard of them, their "Counting Flowers on the Wall" was a No. 1 hit.

Sponsor	Product or Service	Beneficiary	Comments
Johnny's Auto Sales	used cars	Ray Davis, legendary bluegrass dj on WBMD, Baltimore	Sponsor motto: "The Walking Man's Friend"
Kentucky Fried Chicken and Pizza Hut (Pepsico companies)	fast food	National Bluegrass Talent Contest	Would the purists who complain about this latest "commercialization" of their music 1) please submit affidavits that they have never eaten fried chicken or pizza nor drunk Pepsi in their lives, and 2) establish a non-profit foundation or fund the competition themselves?

FIFTEEN

HEARING (AND WATCHING) THE 'GRASS GROW

Compilations, Videos, Instruments, Virtuosos

If you really watch it close, look at all of it, it makes a powerful music. . . . I have never heard any music I thought would
beat it, myself.

—Bill Monroe

This chapter is about the general. It is also about the specific. If you don't want to spend a pile on recordings by each and every artist, you've come to the right place in the book. And if there's a particular (or peculiar) instrument that you've just *got* to hear more of, ditto.

Bluegrass Compilations

Here are some classic bluegrass collections that are definitely tuneful. One obvious advantage of buying a compilation is that

169

you get a sampler of artists. Something catch your ear, turn your head, or knock your socks off? After rearranging your physiognomy, you can go out and buy more by that artist.

Another major attraction is that such collections are often prime places to find music by great performers whose recordings are out of print or hard to find. Some of the compilations below contain classic tracks by the Greenbriar Boys and the Dillards; fiddlers Benny Martin and Tex Logan; mandolinist Earl Taylor; and banjo pickers Buzz Busby, Allen Shelton, and Ted Lundy.

The All-Night Gang: Bluegrass From Nashville, **Rebel 1693 (contemporary bands from Music City, including the New Kentucky Colonels, the Bluegrass Idles, the Sidemen)**

The Best of Sugar Hill Gospel Volume 1: Every Time I Feel the Spirit, **Sugar Hill 9102 (includes Doyle Lawson and Quicksilver, Hot Rize, Skaggs and Rice, the Whites, Seldom Scene)**

Blue Ribbon Bluegrass, **Rounder CAN11 (includes Alison Krauss, J. D. Crowe, Ricky Skaggs, Bela Fleck, David Grisman)**

Bluegrass Spectacular, **CTS 55424 (1950s Starday bluegrass, including Buzz Busby and Jim Eanes)**

Bluegrass at Newport, 1959–1963, **Vanguard 121/2 (includes Flatt and Scruggs, Mac Wiseman, Jim and Jesse, Tex Logan)**

The Festival Tapes: Fourth Annual Telluride Bluegrass and Country Festival, **Flying Fish 068 (from Colorado's newgrass answer to Woodstock; includes New Grass Revival, Peter Rowan, Doc and Merle Watson, Bryan Bowers, John Hartford)**

50 Years of Bluegrass Hits, Volumes 1, 2, 3, 4, **CMH-1777, 9003, 9034, 9035, 9036 (latter-year recordings, mostly from the 1970s, of Lester Flatt, the Osborne Brothers, Jim and Jesse, Mac Wiseman, and others)**

Goin' Up Copper Creek, **Copper Creek 0112 (recently recorded material includes Ralph Stanley, Johnson Mountain Boys, Gary and Jim Brewer, Rickey Watson, plus a spectrum of brother duets and string bands.)**

Heartland Sampler, Heartland 514

High Lonesome: The Story of Bluegrass Music, CMH 8007 (soundtrack from the documentary released in 1994 [see video listings, below]; includes Bill Monroe and His Blue Grass Boys, Stanley Brothers, Jimmy Martin, Seldom Scene, New Deal String Band, and Kenny Kosek; includes some tracks going back to 1951)

Live! At McClure, Rebel 1118 (Ralph Stanley and guests at his annual festival)

Mountain Music Bluegrass Style, Smithsonian Folkways 40038 (influential 1959 collection produced by Mike Seeger; includes Chubby Anthony, Don Stover, Tex Logan, Earl Taylor, and the Stoney Mountain Boys)

Newport Folk Festival 1963–1966—Bluegrass Breakdown, Vanguard 77006 (includes Bill Monroe and His Blue Grass Boys, the Stanley Brothers, the Dillards, the Greenbriar Boys, the New York City Ramblers, Lue and Byron Berline, Fiddling Arthur Smith, Clayton McMichen)

The Possum Tapes, Fat Dog 777 (includes Jim and Jesse, Jimmy Martin, Glen Duncan, Tim O'Brien, Carl Jackson)

Rounder Bluegrass 1, Rounder 11511 (includes Bill Keith, the New Kentucky Colonels, the Bailey Brothers)

Rounder Bluegrass 2, Rounder 11512 (includes the Johnson Mountain Boys, Bela Fleck, Jerry Douglas)

Shine, Hallelujah, Shine, Volumes 1/2/3, Hay Holler Harvest 201/2/3 (Gospel featuring Dudley Connell, Butch Robbins, Larry Stephenson, Dave McLaughlin, and others)

The Stained Glass Hour: Bluegrass and Old-Timey Gospel Music, Rounder 11563 (includes J. D. Crowe and the New South, Johnson Mountain Boys, Delia Bell and Bill Grant, Joe Val and the New England Bluegrass Boys, the Bluegrass Album Band, Boone Creek with Ricky Skaggs, Hazel Dickens, Louvin Brothers, David Grisman, Don Stover, Blue Sky Boys)

The Best of Sugar Hill Gospel Volume 2: Way Down Deep in My Soul, Sugar Hill 9103 (includes Lawson and Quicksilver, Bluegrass Cardinals, Country Gentlemen, Boone Creek, Doc Watson)

20 Bluegrass Originals—Hymns, DL-7911 (includes the Lewis Family, Jimmy Martin, Carl Story)

20 Bluegrass Originals—Instrumentals, DL-7908 (includes Flatt and Scruggs, the Stanley Brothers)

Wild and Reckless Men: Mountain Music Collection, CMH 8002 (theme collection about ramblers, gamblers, and outlaws with fairly recent material by Lester Flatt, the Osbornes, Grandpa Jones, Mac Wisemen, the Bluegrass Cardinals, plus older recordings by the Carter Family, Wade Mainer, and Riley Puckett)

The Third Winterhawk Scholarship Album, Gordo 006 (recently recorded contemporary bluegrass; includes Northern Lights, Matt Glaser, Seldom Scene, Tony Trischka, Tim O'Brien, Warrior River Boys, Jody Stecher and Kate Brislin, Doyle Lawson, Red Knuckles and the Trail Blazers, the Fox Family, Eddie Adcock, Peter Rowan, Dry Branch Fire Squad)

Bluegrass Performances on Video

OK, bluegrass may not have rock-n-roll pyrotechnics (not yet, anyway). But it's still a visually enjoyable art form. Some of the best is being committed to tape and what follows is an extremely incomplete list. One highly recommended program is the intelligent and lovingly assembled documentary *High Lonesome,* which contains incredible archival footage of 1950s and '60s bands when bluegrass was an underground music with a cult following.

Bill Monroe: Father of Bluegrass Music, Original Cinema (as featured on The Nashville Network; with additional footage in home release)

The Dillards. *A Night in the Ozarks,* AudioLithograph Society

The *Andy Griffith Show* featuring the Dillards, *The Best of The Darlings,* United Artists Video 5584 (episodes from the popular TV show)

High Lonesome: The Story of Bluegrass Music, National Entertainment Network/Sanachie Entertainment (Rachel Liebling, producer/director)

Muleskinner. *Muleskinner Live,* **Sierra SHV1001 (California TV special circa 1970 featuring Richard Greene, David Grisman, Bill Keith, Peter Rowan, and Clarence White)**

Various artists. *Banjo Meltdown,* **Tennessee Banjo Institute (video souvenir of a mega banjo instructional camp)**

————. *The 1992 Merle Watson Memorial Festival,* **Wilkes Community College, Wilkesboro, NC (many top acts)**

Bluegrass Auteurs: Who Wrote the Songs?

> Goethe said there would be little left of him if he were to discard what he owed to others.
>
> **—Charlotte Cushman, author**

Some years ago I was in a bar, sitting back and enjoying the music of a good bluegrass club band, when the guitarist/MC plumb ruined my evening.

"The next number we're going to do," he announced, "is a Seldom Scene song called 'My Little Georgia Rose.'"

I snorted in the Coca Cola I had been nursing all evening. The hot banjo introduction that would ordinarily have made me smile only set me scowling. Yes, "My Little Georgia Rose" was featured on a then-popular new album by the Washington, D.C.-based Seldom Scene. But the song was one of the most popular ever written by the Father of Bluegrass himself, Bill Monroe.

This is hardly an isolated case. Bluegrass scholar Robert Cantwell recalls a folk duo at the 1980 National Folk Festival introducing Bill Monroe's "On and On" as an old song whose origins were unknown to them. "In utter defiance of copyright laws," observed Cantwell, " 'On and On' had entered 'tradition'—at the ripe old age of about twenty-seven."

These gaffes are on a level of someone hearing a New York Philharmonic recording of Beethoven's Fifth and enthusing over what a great job Leonard Bernstein had done composing that symphony.

It was also not uncommon in the early days for bandleaders—in jazz and country-western music as well as bluegrass—to purchase rights to a song or assume rights for a song written by one of their band-member employees. An outstanding example in bluegrass is the simple but elegant fiddle tune "The Gold Rush," composed in the mid-1960s by then-Blue Grass Boy Byron Berline, purchased by Monroe, and published under Monroe's name.

The notion of bluegrass as a "traditional" music further murks up the stream of composition credit, as witness one of the most famous tunes in bluegrass history: "Dueling Banjos."

When Warner Brothers was in pre-production on the 1973 movie version of James Dickey's powerful novel Deliverance, a song was sought that could be performed in the movie. Dickey had heard a tape of the instrumental "Dueling Banjos" ten years earlier and recommended it to the producers. They liked the idea and the piece proved a brilliant choice. Instead of two banjos challenging each other back and forth, in the movie a guitar-picking city slicker and a banjo-playing mountain boy exchange riffs on their instruments. After this lovely little jam session, the friendly businessman tries to introduce himself to the retarded youth, who only turns away: a chilling preview of the brutal realities awaiting the vacationers among the beauty of the hills.

Two longtime New York pickers and studio aces, banjoist Eric Weissberg and guitarist Steve Mandell, recorded "Dueling Banjos" for the soundtrack. It became a huge hit in its own right, stimulating national interest in bluegrass. An early banjo album by Weissberg and Marshall Brickman (a banjoist and comedy writer later known for his collaborations with Woody Allen) called New Dimensions in Banjo and Bluegrass was dusted off, given the new recordings of "Dueling Banjos" and a variation titled "End of a Dream," and released as the movie soundtrack album (Warner Brothers BS-2683). Because "Dueling Banjos" was innocently thought to be a traditional tune in the public domain, Weissberg listed himself as composer/arranger on the BMI (Broadcast Music International) forms to collect royalties, a perfectly legal and acceptable practice in the case of an old folk tune.

The problem was, "Dueling Banjos" was not an old, traditional folk tune. Yes, numerous bluegrass bands had recorded it over the years under such titles as "Duelin' Banjos" and "Mockin' Banjos." But by any other name it was still "Feudin' Banjos," composed by Arthur Smith of North Carolina and copyrighted in 1955. Smith had originally recorded it on 4-string tenor banjo, "feuding" with friend and 5-string banjo great Don Reno. When informed, Warner Brothers offered Smith a settlement, reportedly $20,000.

Unbeknownst to Warner executives, Arthur Smith (no relation to this author) was not an old farmer but an established musician and composer, at the time producing Johnny Cash's weekly radio program and appearing on his own syndicated TV show. In court, Smith and Reno picked the tune for the judge (to His Honor's great amusement) and Warner Brothers gave in. Smith got 50 percent of the profits Warners had made on its recording to that date (making him an estimated $200,000 richer overnight), future composer's royalties, plus the reward he deserved as creator of what had been voted the 1973 BMI Country Song of the Year.

And everyone (including some other bands who were contacted by Smith's lawyers) was reminded that not everything in bluegrass is old as the hills.

Take Your Pick: The Best of the Bluegrass Instrumentalists

BANJO

> If it ain't got a banjo, it ain't bluegrass.
> —attributed to Hub Nitche, founder of *Banjo Newsletter*

We are living in the age of sick banjo jokes. What's the difference between a banjo and a chain saw? Answer: The chain saw has more dynamic range. How can you tell if the stage a banjo player is standing on is level? Answer: The drool comes out both sides of his mouth. What do you call five thousand banjos sunk in the Mariana Trench? Answer: A start.

Sorry. No more banjo jokes. The banjo has an ancient history, having doubtless derived from West African instruments that used a large carved gourd as a resonator. Some slave ship captains were happy to have Africans bring their folk instruments to divert themselves and the crew during long voyages, and the instrument was introduced into the plantations of the ante-bellum South where it was known as the "banza" or "banjar."

In the West Indies it was the "merrywang." We can only ponder how far bluegrass would have developed if, on the Grand Ole Opry in 1945, Bill Monroe had introduced his new discovery Earl Scruggs, the three-finger merrywang picker.

Sorry again. Anyway, the banjo became a popular instrument in the South. Along the way, a drum-like resonator replaced the gourd. Research into ancient playing styles suggests that the reason for this went beyond making the banjo louder. The original West African technique probably involved strumming the strings and tapping the top of the instrument in rapid succession. Thus the banjo seems to have originally been both a stringed *and* a percussion instrument. Older banjos were fretless like a violin, but later instruments gained frets like a guitar.

The folk version of the instrument had five strings, the fifth being a drone that ran halfway up the neck on the side facing up to the player. Joel Walker Sweeney, a minstrel, has traditionally been credited with adding the fifth string but recent research suggests that African-Americans developed it, or credit may even belong to their forebears. Whoever invented it, the fifth string became vital to the folk sound because of the pinging accompaniment it gave the instrument.

The fact that the 5-string was recognized as the original banjo is reflected in the model numbering used by the Gibson company (manufacturer of the "Mastertone," for years the instrument of choice for bluegrass pickers). In its catalogs, Gibson designated jazz and Dixieland-style plectrum-strummed 4-string banjos as its "TB" or tenor banjo series, but the 5-strings were labeled "RB" for regular banjo.

The instrument was immortalized in Stephen Foster's "Ring, Ring the Banjo" as the source of "that good old song." But as popular as it had been in the lowlands it did not gain wide use in the southern mountains until the late nineteenth century. In the mountains, the violin known to the English and Scots-Irish settlers had long been favored. The fiddle was sufficient as a solo instrument to accompany singing and dancing, just as it had been for centuries in the British Isles. But once the banjo and fiddle were played together, listeners quickly appreciated how well the banjo provided chording and rhythm backup for the arpeggios. It was a rudimentary string band. Indeed, Flatt and Scruggs were fond of presenting fiddle and banjo duets on their shows, explaining that in parts of North Carolina and eastern Tennessee just the two instruments constituted a band. (The addition of a guitar made for a *big* band.)

Meanwhile, in towns and cities, a so-called "classical" finger-

33. Tony Trischka (photo by Gregory Heisler).

picking style among turn-of-the-century musicians, notably Vess Ossman and Fred Van Epps, who recorded for Thomas Edison's cylinder records, a variety of marches, dances, and pop tunes played on the banjo.

The instrument moved off the porch and out of the parlor and onto the bandstand. It needed to be louder. Gibson and other manufacturers perfected formidable systems of large drum bodies containing tone rings and backed by resonators to project the sound to maximum effect.

Before bluegrass, the predominant picking methods were frailing (in which the thumb sounds the fifth string drone while the backs of the fingernails pick out melody notes and strum accompaniment) and double thumbing (a thumb and single finger technique in which the thumb sounds much of the melody). The three-finger styles allowed greater power, speed, and versatility, especially within a band context.

As mentioned earlier, Snuffy Jenkins, Earl Scruggs, Don Reno and others were products of a North Carolina style of three-finger banjo playing (that, over the years, was probably influenced by the recordings of Ossman and Van Epps and the blues styling of African-American banjo players like Gus Cannon).

A subsequent advance was the so-called "melodic style" perfected independently by Bill Keith of Massachusetts and Bobby Thompson of Tennessee. Using the fluid Scruggs-style three-finger picking patterns, the melodic players developed fretting hand strategies that allowed them to play straight melody lines with no (or few) rhythm notes. The initial benefit of the new style came in playing the exact melodies of old fiddle tunes. Previously, Scruggs-style pickers could usually only approximate fiddle tune melodies, although this worked fine because banjo solos functioned as variations on the theme. Obviously a powerful straight melodic style could lead to other things. And it did, to the playing of chromatic lines and jazz-like improvisations, facilitating the blend of bluegrass, jazz, and rock known today as newgrass.

Keith also made a hardware contribution by helping to perfect a type of tuning peg that would allow returning banjo strings in quick, discreet, and accurate intervals. As Earl Scruggs had discovered, this not only allowed fast changes from G to D tuning between songs; you could also retune up and down *during* the songs, and he did in the instrumentals "Flint Hill Special" and "Randy Lynn Rag." If you're having a tough time hearing this in your mind's ear, think of these Keith-Scruggs tuners as, like, wah-wah pedals for the banjo. Scruggs had to screw a home-made contraption to the head of his banjo to accomplish this, but Keith engineered a way to include a cam system inside tuners that would just fit in the existing peg holes.

Several greats of bluegrass banjo were mentioned in the chapters on major bands, sidemen, and styles: Earl Scruggs, Ralph Stanley, Don Reno, J. D. Crowe, Bill Keith, Bobby Thompson, and Tony Trischka. It's interesting to note that all have received the ultimate kudo of having their names now associated with a distinctive approach to the instrument: original "gold standard" picking ("Scruggs-style"); swift basic picking with an aggressive edge ("Crowe-style"); old-timey flavored ("Stanley-style"); bouncy three-finger picking augmented with jazzy passages ("Reno-style"); flowing melodic lines ("Keith-" or "Thompson-style"); chromatic and experimental lines with accented passages ("Trischka-style").

Several masters of traditional-style bluegrass 5-string are worth your attention: banjo heroes of the 1950s and '60s, many of whom remain active (Bill Emerson, Doug Dillard, Vic Jordan, Allen Shelton, Raymond Fairchild); great cult figures who should not be forgotten (Johnny Whisnant); talents who began expanding the 5-string's horizons while providing the drive for the next generation of bluegrass bands (Alan Munde, Raymond McLain, Carl Jackson, Chris Warner); and the great contemporary instrumentalists (Tom Adams, Alison Brown, John Hickman, Pete Wernick).

Some pickers are continuing to push the envelope of what you can do on the old cheesecutter (Bela Fleck, Dennis Cyporyn, Marty Cutler, Tony Furtado). In an exciting development, some players (notably Trischka and Stephen Wade) are delving back into the instrument's past, dramatically bringing the music's roots to life by recording along with ancient West African or Celtic instruments, thus becoming the ultimate traditionalists and bringing the banjo full circle in the process.

And that's no joke.

Eddie Adcock and Don Reno. *Sensational Twin Banjos,* Rebel
  1482

Tom Adams. *Right Hand Man,* Rounder 0282

Area Code 615. *Trip in the Country,* Polydor 24-4025 (featuring
  Bobby Thompson on banjo)

Alison Brown. *Simple Pleasures,* Vanguard 79459

J. D. Crowe. *Blackjack,* Rebel 1583

Douglas Cyporyn. *I Must Be Dreaming,* Krypton 0014

Doug Dillard. *The Banjo Album,* Sierra 6008

Bill Emerson. *Gold Plated Banjo,* Rebel 1671

Raymond Fairchild. *Me and My Banjo at Home in Maggie Valley,* Atteiram 1655

Lester Flatt, Earl Scruggs, and the Foggy Mountain Boys.
  Foggy Mountain Banjo, Columbia 1564

Bela Fleck. *Crossing the Tracks,* Rounder 0121

———. *Deviation,* Rounder 0196 (backed by New Grass Revival)

Tony Furtado. *Within Reach,* Rounder 0290

John Hickman. *Don't Mean Maybe,* Rounder 0101

Bill Keith. *Banjoistics,* Rounder 0148

———. *Beating Around the Bush,* Green Linnet 2107

Carl Jackson. *Banjo Hits!,* Sugar Hill 3737

Vic Jordan. *Pickaway,* Atteriram 1027

Ted Lundy, Bob Paisley, and the Southern Mountain Boys.
  Lovesick and Sorrow, Rounder 0107

Raymond McLain. *A Place of My Own,* Flying Fish 70597

Alan Munde. *Banjo Sandwich,* Ridgerunner 0001

———. *Blue Ridge Express,* Rounder 0301

———. *Festival Favorites Revisited,* Rounder 0311

Larry Perkins. *A Touch of the Past,* Pinecastle 1022

Don Reno and Bobby Thompson. *Banjo Bonanza,* Reader's
  Digest RDA-096/D (a 1983 album featuring twin banjo
  arrangements—by two all-time greats—of "Foggy Mountain Breakdown," "Rocky Top," "Dueling Banjos," and
  other 5-string hits. At 500,000 in sales, this curiosity may ac-

tually be one of the greatest selling bluegrass records of all time!)

Don Reno, Red Smiley, and the Tennessee Cutups. *Instrumentals,* King 552

Allen Shelton. *Shelton Special,* Rounder 0088

Tony Trischka. *Banjoland,* Rounder 0087

———. *Dust on The Needle,* Rounder 11508

Chris Warner. *Chris Warner and Friends,* Webco 0132

Eric Weissberg. *Dueling Banjos: Music from the Movie Deliverance,* Warner Brothers 2683 (with Marshall Brickman, Steve Mandell, and others; most previously released several years before as *New Dimensions in Banjo and Bluegrass*)

Pete Wernick. *Dr. Banjo Steps Out,* Flying Fish 046

Johnnie Whisnant. *Johnnie Whisnant,* Rounder 0038

Various artists. *American Banjo Three-Finger and Scruggs Style,* Smithsonian/Folkways 40037 (reissue of another classic collection; includes Dewitt "Snuffy" Jenkins, Smiley Hobbs, and Junie Scruggs, Earl's older brother)

———. *Rounder Banjo,* Rounder 11524 (includes J. D. Crowe, Allen Shelton, Herb Pederson, Marty Cutler, Don Stover, Paul Silvious, Ted Lundy, Butch Robins, Lamar Grier, Tony Trishcka)

———. *Rounder Banjo Extravaganza, Live,* Rounder 0296 (Tom Adams, Tony Furtado, and Tony Trischka)

FIDDLE

> The violinist is that particularly human phenomenon distilled to a rare potency—half tiger, half poet.
> —Yehudi Menuhin, violin virtuoso

Some music historians believe that the modern violin was perfected about 1550 and in popularity soon replaced the bagpipes (which in various forms had been a popular if cumbersome instrument throughout Europe and the Middle East). It was brought over to America by Anglo- and Scots-Irish settlers as a portable form of entertainment.

Those who look with concern on the effect of rock-n-roll on social mores should know that even before jazz and other forms of "Negro music" were being accused of corrupting youth, the fiddle was being condemned from eighteenth and early nineteenth century pulpits as being "the devil's box." Indeed, it was rumored that certain fanatical fiddlers sold their souls to Satan to obtain great musical powers. (This tradition may have inspired the popular fiddle tune "Devil's Dream." That number, incidentally, was one of the first instrumentals that Bill Keith recorded in 1963 with Bill Monroe using the new melodic style of banjo picking. As far as I know, however, Keith's ever-present cap does not hide a pair of horns.) The fiddle became a popular pairing with the banjo in mountain music and, later, in the early commercial string bands with banjo, guitar, and mandolin.

Bill Monroe, of course, loved the instrument, especially as played by his Uncle Pen Vandiver. He featured it in his band from the first and even tried to reproduce elements of his Uncle Pen's bow shuffle in his mandolin playing. (I have it on good authority that Monroe wanted to be a fiddler himself, but his eldest brother Birch got dibs on the family fiddle and when Bill was finally able to practice with it, his siblings teased him so much—with such constructive comments as "If you don't stop looking sourer than you're playing that thing, you're going to kill us all"—that he gave up and concentrated on the mandolin.)

Because of the fiddle's importance to bluegrass, it's worth considering its greatest masters in some detail.

As exciting as the fiddling of Gid Tanner, Clayton McMichen, John Carson, and other old-time string band greats was, modern bluegrass style has less in common with the stereotyped hillbilly "sawin' on a string" and more with the smooth, "long bow" techniques of later country players. Kenny Baker, who had the longest tenure with Bill Monroe, is especially known for his very active but smooth bowing (and his disdain for northerners who think that short, choppy, back-and-forth bowing is bluegrass fiddling, calling it "that Yankee bowing").

That's not to say that a more primal old-time sound was left

34. Scott Stoneman (courtesy of Pattie Murphy).

out of bluegrass. Curly Ray Cline, as Ralph Stanley's fiddler, was highly successful with his shuffling, somewhat old-time sound. Paul Warren, who had the longest tenure with Flatt and Scruggs, also had an exciting hoe-down style and played flowing leads and almost lilting backup.

Of the true pioneers of bluegrass fiddling, Chubby Wise is venerated for his bluesy, emotionally expressive playing and sweet tone, which made him a perfect match with early Bill Monroe. Benny Martin could get into the rarified realms of third position (and higher) playing with double stops on the neck of his fiddles but also had a great drive, which made him a perfect match with early Earl Scruggs.

Early pedal steel guitar players patterned themselves after fiddlers, so naturally fiddlers would start listening to pedal steel players. The influential Vassar Clements regularly rolls out slick solos using double and even triple stop positions (in which he was much influenced by the playing of Texas swing legend Dale Potter) and also adds elements of what can only be called hillbilly bop.

Scotty Stoneman presented sliding, shaking, double stop, bluesy fiddling with an almost brassy tone that was attention-getting and greatly influenced the playing of Richard Greene, who combined it with his orchestral-quality technique for very fine results.

Of contemporary players, Byron Berline has mastered elements of the studied but lively Texas "contest" style of fiddling while having exciting bluegrass technique. Stuart Duncan and Mark O'Connor are the epitome of modern seamless, well-sculpted, state-of-the-art playing that still offers soulful surprises. O'Connor, probably the most talked about fiddler in years, brings to his musicianship the tonal colors and gorgeous playing that made him perhaps the greatest young contest fiddler ever.

Today the fiddle is enjoying renewed popularity in Nashville, as witness the playing of Blaine Sprouse, Glen Duncan, Bobby Hicks (another great bluegrass and Texas swing double master), and Alison Krauss. Bluegrass veterans Jimmy Shumate, Jimmy Buchanan, and Buddy Spicher are loved for the wonderful bluegrass soul that streams from their bows.

Kenny Baker. *Master Fiddler,* County 2705 (selected recordings from 1968 to 1983)

—— and Howdy Forrester. *Red Apple Rag,* County 784

—— and Bobby Hicks. *Darkness on the Delta,* County 782

—— and Blaine Sprouse. *Indian Springs,* Rounder 0259

Byron Berline. *Dad's Favorites,* Rounder 0100 (old and contest-style tunes)

——. *Outrageous,* Flying Fish 227

Jimmy Buchanan. *To Love And Live Together,* CEO 9204-SP

Sen. Robert Byrd. *Mountain Fiddler,* County 769 (Yes, the former Senate majority leader is a solid player. During one election an opponent made fun of Byrd's hobby and immediately lost big points in the polls, showing that in West Virginia you can criticize a man's politics but don't you dare mock his music.)

Vassar Clements. *Grass Routes,* Rounder 0287

——. *The Bluegrass Session,* Flying Fish 038

Curly Ray Cline. *Fox Hunter,* Old Homestead 90142

Glen Duncan. *Sweet Water,* Turquoise 5061

Stuart Duncan. *Stuart Duncan,* Rounder 0263

Richard Greene. *The Greene Fiddler,* Sierra 6005

Bobby Hicks. *Texas Crapshooter,* County 2706 (one side bluegrass-style, one side Western-style)

Dick Kimmel. *Wild Turkey Rag,* Copper Creek 0115

Kenny Kosek and Matt Glaser. *Hasty Lonesome,* Rounder 0127

Alison Krauss. *Too Late To Cry,* Rounder 0235

Benny Martin. *The Fiddle Collection,* CMH 9006

Joe Meadows. *Fiddle Instrumentals with Country Ham,* Vetco-531

Mark O'Connor. *The Championship Years,* Country Music Foundation 15 (amazing recordings by O'Connor while a wunderkind blue-ribbon winner at major fiddle contests)

——. *Soppin' the Gravy,* Rounder 0137

Jimmy Shumate. *Buckle Up the Backstrap,* **Heritage 106**
Benny Sims. *Fiddle Favorites,* **0091**
Buddy Spicher. *Fiddle Classics,* **Flying Fish 278**
Blaine Sprouse. *Brillancy,* **Rounder 0209**
Art Stamper. *It's a Dilly,* **Old Homestead 90191**
Scotty Stoneman. *The Lost Masters,* **Old Homestead 90202**
————. *Live in L.A. with the Kentucky Colonels,* **Sirra 4206**
Chubby Wise. *Chubby Returns to Nashville,* **Pinecone 1031**
Various artists. *Rounder Fiddle,* **Rounder 11565 (includes Glen Duncan, Eddie Stubbs, Ricky Skaggs, Sam Bush)**
————. *The World's Greatest Country Fiddlers,* **CMH 5904 (includes Paul Warren, Benny Martin, Kenny Baker, Buddy Spicher)**

MANDOLIN

Hearing in the distance
Two mandolins like creatures in the dark
Creating the agony of ecstasy.
                              —George Barker, British poet

The mandolin has a heroic role in bluegrass, but its odyssey to fulfill its destiny was unlikely indeed.

The mandolin was a favorite European instrument in the eighteenth and early nineteenth centuries. Beethoven, Vivaldi, and other great masters composed for it. In the late 1800s, the mandolin found huge popularity in America. It blended well with the guitar, and both were suitable instruments for parlor entertainment. Perhaps because of its powers as a "courting" instrument, it became the rage on college campuses, where banjos, mandolins, and guitars joined in music club bands long before they were united in bluegrass. Entire mandolin orchestras performed in concert halls. And why not? Just as there is a violin family of instruments—violin, viola, cello, and bass—there is a mandolin family of mandolin, mandola, mandocello, and mandobass. The entire group has experienced a recurrence of popularity thanks to the acoustic music boom.

For quite some time, the predominant instrument was the Italian-style mandolin, whose rounded back was constructed of lengthwise strips of wood. Alternate light and dark strips were often used (giving such instruments the appearance of potato-boring beetles; hence the nickname in the South, " 'tater bug mandolins"). As an improvement, a cabinet maker in Kalamazoo, Michigan named Orville Gibson created mandolins with violin-like tops and backs, lengthened necks, plus a "cutaway" in the lower half of the body that allowed players to finger very high notes. Gibson had improved the playability, but the real breakthroughs were the violin-style tops and backs with special interior carving to give the best frequency responses (a process known as "voicing"). The Gibson mandolin sounded better and sounded louder. The cabinet maker was on his way to founding one of the most important musical instrument companies in America. (Incidentally, most early luthiers of this era were also cabinet makers, although not exactly in the same way that many early doctors were bloodletting barbers.)

Gibson had his new patented invention. But as Orville and Wilbur Wright showed us, it takes two to make an invention really fly. Joining craftsman Orville Gibson as acoustic engineer of his growing Gibson Guitar and Mandolin Company was Lloyd Loar, who perfected the voicing and internal construction of the mandolins. The F-5 series Gibsons of 1921–1924 with internal labels singed by Mr. Loar are considered among the best ever made and are certainly the most expensive.

It was a 1923 vintage F-5 Lloyd Loar mandolin that Bill Monroe came across one day in the 1930s in the window of a Florida barber shop, sale price $150. This was an "F-hole" model, with top openings like a fiddle. Mandolins with round, guitar-like sound holes have been built by Gibson and other manufacturers. Indeed, the European designs typically employed the round hole configuration. But the F-holed Gibson was ideal for Monroe's purposes. Of course with its flat back it was easier to hold steady while standing up. But it was the sound too: a sweet tone for tender tremolos, a loud bark for rhythm strumming, and a bright halo around individual notes. It could hold its own against arching fiddles, large-bodied rhythm guitars, and be-resonatored banjos. It could cut through the sound of a whole band. What Orville Gibson had intended for concert halls was going to become—in the strong, work-hardened hands of Bill Monroe—a voice of authority.

Needless to say, bluegrass mandolin has never been for shrinking violets, a garlanded instrument over which to exchange shy glances in a darkened parlor. Even though it had its place in old-timey bands, it assumed a whole new role after Bill Monroe wedded fiddle and blues guitar stylings to the instrument.

One of the most publicly underrated mandolinists, who is held in high regard by other musicians, is Hershel Sizemore, whose albums with the Shenandoah Cutups are classics and who returned to bluegrass in recent years with a highly regarded comeback album.

John Duffey, formerly with the original Country Gentlemen and of late with the Seldom Scene, has developed a mandolin style as large, original, and outrageous as his personality. Jimmy Gaudreau, who replaced Duffey in the Gentlemen, more than filled his predecessor's shoes. The playing of this former rock lead guitarist is a model of clean but lively musicianship. Following Gaudreau was Doyle Lawson, who has achieved a seamless blend of traditional bluegrass and uptown country 'grass picking.

Red Rector, although recalled as a former partner of Bill Clifton and a real traditionalist, was actually one of the most innovative pickers to hold the instrument. Roland White honed his talents playing with his late brother Clarence, a now-legendary guitarist, and showcased them as a member of the Country Gazette and as a solo artist. Butch Baldassari is highly recognized as a Nashville-based picker and as a dedicated mandolin teacher.

Ricky Skaggs, now known by most audiences as a superstar of the new country music, started his musical career as a bluegrass mandolinist and he's still one of the most pleasing and exciting players you could ever listen to. His friend and in-law Buck

35. Doyle Lawson (courtesy of Doyle Lawson).

White gets more attention as father and musical partner to his daughters, but Buck's western-swing-influenced mandolin stylings are just a delight.

Like the banjo and fiddle, the mandolin has been a vehicle for some wild and wonderful experimentations. The great acoustic jazz of violinist Stephane Grapelli, guitarist Django Reinhardt, and their Quintet of the Hot Club of France had an impact on modern mandolin music when it reached the ears of David Grisman, a New Yorker now based in California. Grisman helped blend bluegrass and jazz into what is now generically known as "new acoustic music." (His own brand is lovingly called "Dawg" music for the initials of David W. Grisman.)

Another New Yorker, Andy Statman, became the Charlie Parker of bluegrass mandolin during tenures with the newgrass bands Country Cooking and Breakfast Special. No wonder he was once quoted as declaring, "There are no wrong notes, only poor choices." But no matter what multi-tonic directions he takes, Statman demonstrates impeccable timing and technique. He is also an exceptional McReynolds-style crosspicker and has written an instructional book on the style.

While the New Yorkers were making their experiments, down in Louisville mandolinist Sam Bush of the New Grass Revival was making his. When he cuts loose with his scales, the scales fall from your eyes on what the instrument can do. Yet Bush does not display technique for its own sake, instead bringing true musicianship to even the most bravado performances. Peter Ostroushko similarly displays a blend of adventurousness and good taste in his exceptional playing.

A major influence on Grisman, Bush, and a generation of hot pickers was Jethro Burns, better know for his contributions to the country comedy team of Homer and Jethro but one of the most astonishing mandolin players ever.

A true individualist is Niles Hokkanen. A Florida native, his influences range from Bill Monroe to Frank Zappa to his own fevered imagination. Hokkanen first burst onto the scene as a mandolin theorist with detailed instruction books on progressive players and advanced techniques. From there, appearances on National Public Radio's "A Prairie Home Companion" firmly

36. Jerry Douglas (photo by Peter Nash).

established his reputation as a no-limits picker. If the mandolin is his spaceship and bluegrass his original rocket fuel, Hokkanen is now traveling through the music of the spheres.

Mike Marshall has achieved tremendous virtuosity and channeled it into projects from new acoustic music to jazz to mandolin chamber quartets. A player with a beautiful touch and expression on the instrument is Barry Mitterhoff, formerly of the Bottle Hill and Skyline bands. His talents and interests are so eclectic that he plays bluegrass, jazz, classical, South American and even Hollywood music on it with ease. (His medleys of tunes from *The Wizard of Oz* is now a legendary showpiece.) Radim Zenkel's use of bluegrass, acoustic jazz, and Eastern European folk modes in creating his beautifully textured style has won him the praise of fans and fellow mandolinists alike. And 13-year-old Chris Thile promises to be the next superstar of the bluegrass mandolin.

Bridging the gap between Monroe and the planet Saturn is Frank Wakefield. A former partner of Red Allen, Wakefield was one of the first traditional-style bluegrass mandolinists to start going into musical orbits. Once heard (or seen), Wakefield is not soon forgotten.

Butch Baldassari. *Old Town,* Rebel 1681
Jethro Burns and Red Rector. *Old Friends,* Rebel 1626
Sam Bush. *Late as Usual,* Rounder 0195
David Grisman. *Dawg '90,* Acoustic Disc 1
————. *Hot Dawg,* AandM 3292
Niles Hokkanen. *On Fire and Ready!,* Mandocrucian 003
Doyle Lawson. *Tennessee Dream,* Rebel 4305
Jesse McReynolds. *Mandolin Workshop,* Hill 202
Mike Marshall. *Gator Strut,* Rounder 0208 (with Darol Anger)
Barry Mitterhoff. *Silk City,* Flying Fish 472
Mick Moloney. *Strings Attached,* Green Linnet 1027
Bill Monroe. *Classic Bluegrass Instrumentals,* Rebel 850
Bobby Osborne. *Bobby and His Mandolin,* CMH 6256
Peter Ostroushko. *Blue Mesa,* Redhouse 30

Red Rector and Norman Blake. *Guitar and Mandolin Duets,* **County 755**

Hershel Sizemore. *Bounce Away,* **Rebel 4308**

——. *Back in Business,* **Hay Holler Harvest 105**

Andy Statman. *Nashville Mornings, New York Nights,* **Rounder 0174**

Chris Thile. *Leading Off,* **Sugar Hill 3828**

——. *A Day in the Country,* **Pinecastle 1028**

Frank Wakefield and Red Allen. *The Kitchen Tapes,* **AC 11**

Buck White. *Buck White and the Down Home Folks,* **County 735**

Roland White. *Trying to Get to You,* **Sugar Hill 3826**

Various artists. *Early Mandolin Classics,* **Rounder 1050 (includes Gid Tanner and the Skillet Lickers and other string bands)**

Radim Zenkel. *Czech It Out,* **Acoustic Disc 12**

DOBRO

> I bought my first Dobro from Buck Graves in 1961—the first day after getting back from our honeymoon. My wife has never let me forget it. . . .
> —Mike Auldridge to interviewer Bobby Wolfe

The name "dobro" was first coined as a trade name for a brand of resophonic guitar (basically an acoustic guitar with a self-contained metal resonator). The National Instrument Company and other manufacturers have created similar instruments. These guitars can be fretted and many blues fingerpickers love the sound they get from them. But it's more common for the dobro's action (the space between the strings and the fretboard) to be raised so the instrument can be played with a metal slide in the fretting hand in what is known as "Hawaiian" or "bottleneck" style.

African-American musicians developed methods of tuning their guitars to open chords, then using a flat hard object like a pocket knife or the neck of a glass bottle to slide along the strings. (The necks were carefully broken off and heated to remove the sharp edges.) The Hawaiians, who got the guitar from Spanish and Portuguese sailors, probably developed their slide style independently of American blues men: for one thing, the islanders turned their guitars 90 degrees and played them on their laps.

The National Instrument Company patented an early resophonic guitar that offered extra amplification without electricity. The first dobro guitar was patented in 1925 by three Eastern European immigrants living in California, the Dopyera brothers (sometimes spelled Dopera). "Dobro" thus stands for "Dopyera Brothers," but there is apparently also a pun on the Slavic word for "good." The instrument was used in country music as early as 1927 and later in western swing. Dobro pioneer Cliff Carlisle is heard on a number of Jimmy Rodgers sides, and Brother Oswald Kirby was a featured member of the band of country music king Roy Acuff.

Later, the ultimate slide guitar was developed: the electrified pedal steel. This versatile instrument began displacing the fiddle in country-and-western bands in the late 1950s and soon its whining, insinuating sound became synonymous with Nashville music.

No wonder Flatt and Scruggs—eager to keep as large a niche in Nashville as possible, wanting a third strong solo instrument, but not particularly enamored of the mandolin—were delighted to seize on Buck Graves' dobrolic talents as a solution to many problems. They quickly switched him from bass (the position for which he was actually first hired) to dobro.

Graves had been inspired by Carlisle (in fact, his "old hound dog" contained parts from Carlisle's instrument). He soon inspired others. Maybe the dobro never became a common instrument in bluegrass, but in certain bands it's been indispensable. Tut Taylor contributed his talents (and part of a name) to John Hartford's Dobrolic Plectral Society band; Stacy Phillips' strutting stylings were integral to the Breakfast Special newgrass band; Mike Auldridge became synonymous with the Seldom

37. Doc Watson (photo by Peter Figen).

Scene; and Jerry Douglas has become nearly indispensable to Nashville studio sessions and to the new acoustic music in general.

Mike Auldridge. *Mike Auldridge,* **Flying Fish 029**
Jerry Douglas. *Fluxology,* **Rounder 0093**
—————. *Slide Rule,* **Sugar Hill 3797**
Buck Graves. *King of the Dobro,* **CMH 6252**
————— **and Kenny Baker.** *Flying South,* **Ridge 0034**
Bashful Brother Oswald (Kirby). *Brother Oswald,* **Rounder 0013**
Gene Wooten. *Gene Wooten Sings and Plays Dobro,* **Pinecastle 1024**
Various artists. *The Great Dobro Sessions,* **Sugar Hill 2206 (includes Buck Graves, Jerry Douglas, Mike Auldridge, Sally Van Meter, Oswald Kirby, Tut Taylor, Gene Wooten, Stacy Phillips)**

GUITAR

> Among God's creatures two, the dog and the guitar, have taken all sizes and shapes, in order not to be separated from the man.
>
> —Andres Segovia, guitar virtuoso

Rhythm guitar has been part of bluegrass since the beginning and even before. But as a lead instrument, the guitar came into its own in the 1960s with the influence of Arthel "Doc" Watson of Deep Gap, North Carolina.

Doc Watson is a remarkable man. He once completely rewired his home, his work passing inspection on the first go-round. He has installed an electric garage door opener for his wife, repaired the stereo system in his band's travel camper, adjusted the TV antenna on his house, and tuned his family's color TV.

Doc Watson has also been blind since early childhood.

This is not the stuff of apocryphal myth. Trustworthy eyewitnesses have independently testified as to the truth of all this. Doc personally told me that electronics would have been his profession had he been sighted. I know a blind man adjusting a color TV seems impossible, but the qualification is that it was of the older tube type. The components gave off a detectable and distinctive vibration when they were in tune. Doc modestly admits he can't tune the new generation of sets with solid-state circuitry.

Not surprisingly, the delicate and deft touch of the man from Deep Gap has also produced some of the finest folk music the world has ever heard, bar none. Watson picks heck out of a banjo and is a vocalist who can move you to tears or laughter depending on whether he's singing an ancient ballad or a nonsense ditty. He is a superb fingerpicker. His greatest influence in this style was on the legendary Merle Travis. Doc's son Merle Edward Watson, named for Travis and country singer Eddy Arnold, was also superb and was for years his father's primary accompanist until his 1985 death in a farm tractor accident. One of the nation's premier bluegrass/folk festivals is held each spring in his memory at the Wilkes Community College, Wilkesboro, North Carolina, benefiting educational programs.

But it is as a flatpicking guitarist that Doc has had his greatest influence. People used plectrums to play melodies on guitars before him just as people wrote papers on theoretical physics before Albert Einstein. But Watson's flatpicking had about the same revelatory effect on guitarists that the Special Theory of Relativity had on scientists. The flashy, fluid, jaunty yet versatile and tasteful style of Watson—who could whip off extended guitar runs while casually conversing with the audience—had about the same effect on musicians as seeing time and space bent had on physicists.

Although the guitar was not unknown in the United States in the early 1800s (Andrew Jackson's daughter owned one), it came surprisingly late to the mountains. It is believed to have been seriously introduced into southern music via black laborers who went into the hills to lay tracks for the railroads. Prominent old-time style white musician Hobart Smith once claimed not to have seen his first guitar until about 1917 when he heard one played by a member of a black railroad construction gang laying track near Saltville, Virginia. Blind guitarist Riley Puckett, heavily influenced by black guitarists, brought heavy bass lines to hillbilly music. In all probability it was his powerful work that influenced other string band and bluegrass guitarists.

For bluegrass musicians, largebodied guitars such as the Martin D-28 and D-35 "Dreadnought" series—named after the battleship class—were the instruments of choice: in the early days, in order to be heard during concerts in schoolhouses where there were no PA systems, but later, to compete with loud banjos and fiddles.

Although Doc Watson should not be categorized primarily as a bluegrass guitarist, his influence on the music has been profound. Strumming rhythm and playing melodies with a plectrum was nothing new, but Watson developed a crisp, authoritative flatpicking style that could complement and challenge the best banjo, mandolin, and fiddle work. Although the velocity of Doc's solo showcases can be frightening, he never loses control, clarity, or taste. At the 1963 Newport Folk Festival, he whipped off runs on "Black Mountain Rag" while casually commenting on the weather ("That sun's hot, ain't it?"), completely blowing folk audiences out of their seats and other guitarists out of their cases.

Since then, young flatpickers have wolfed down his riffs as ravenously as aspiring mandolinists have striven to master Monroe's style or banjoists Scruggs' picking. Watson has set high standards for virtuoso playing that never becomes an exercise in cluttered flash, and he balances his instrumentals with presentations of mountain ballads and early country music.

Perhaps the most influential of Doc's admirers have been Tony Rice and Clarence White. Like Watson, Rice picks cleanly and with authority. But thanks in part to playing with David Grisman and other new acoustic musicians, he has developed a jazz-like float over the strings that makes it sound somehow like he's not picking notes out of the instrument but dropping them in so they can flow back out. Once heard, the Rice sound is immediately recognizable. His brother Wyatt, another exceptional guitarist, is also beginning to achieve recognition.

As mentioned in the section on the West Coast, Clarence

White was a member of several robust California bands and joined the Byrds during that rock band's final phase as a country-rock outfit. His innovative stylings will live as long as aspiring guitarists strive to decipher hot licks from great recordings. Other members of the flatpicking pantheon include Norman Blake, a multi-instrumentalist deeply rooted in traditional mountain and folk musics; Dan Crary, recently featured with the progressive bluegrass band California; and newcomer David Grier, a winner of the International Bluegrass Music Association guitarist-of-the-year honors.

Players with devoted followings include former Country Cooking alumnus Russ Barenberg; Wayne Henderson of Appalachia; Bob Harris, recently a mainstay of Vassar Clements' band; and national flatpicking contest winners Steve Kaufmann and Orrin Starr. Eddie Adcock is famous as a banjo picker, but his guitar style is unique and should not be overshadowed or overlooked.

Eddie Adcock. *Eddie Adcock and His Guitar,* **CMH 6265**
Russ Barenberg. *Halloween Rehearsal,* **Rounder 11534**
Norman Blake. *Whiskey Before Breakfast,* **Rounder 0063**
Joe Carr. *Utter Nonsense,* **Ridgerunner 0024**
Dan Crary. *Bluegrass Guitar,* **Sugar Hill 3806**
———. *Jammed If I Do,* **Sugar Hill 3824 (with Watson, Rice, Blake, Gambetta)**
Glenda Faye. *Flatpickin' Favorites,* **Flying Fish 432 (with Bill Monroe, Jesse McReynolds)**
David Grier. *Freewheeling,* **Rounder 0250**
Wayne Henderson. *Rugby Guitar,* **Flying Fish 542**
Steve Kaufman. *The Arkansas Traveler,* **Sleeping Bear, 4894-08**
Joel Mabus. *Flatpick,* **Foss 693**
Tony Rice. *Guitar,* **Rebel 3722**
———. *Tony Rice Plays and Sings Bluegrass,* **Rounder 0253**
Wyatt Rice. *New Market Gap,* **Rounder 0272**
Sandy Rothman and Steve Potter. *Bluegrass Guitar Duets,* **Sierra 6013**

James Alan Shelton. *Blues in the Blue Ridge,* **Heartland 515**

Larry Sparks. *Lonesome Guitar,* **Rebel 1633**

Orrin Starr. *No Frets Barred,* **Flying Fish 267**

Merle Travis. *Folk Songs of the Hills,* **Bear Family 15636**

Doc Watson. *Riding That Midnight Train,* **Sugar Hill 3752**

————. *Portrait,* **Sugar Hill 2204**

————. *My Dear Old Southern Home,* **Sugar Hill 3795**

————. *Elementary Doctor Watson!,* **Sugar Hill 3812**

———— **and Merle Watson.** *Remembering Merle,* **Sugar Hill 3800 (tracks from 1970 to 1976 showcasing Merle)**

Clarence White. *The Kentucky Colonels Featuring Clarence White,* **Rounder 0098**

BASS

Is it not strange that sheep's guts should hole souls out of men's bodies?

—Shakespeare

Okay, the bard was referring to the catgut-stringed violin. But why not apply it to the bass fiddle? The bass is the base of bluegrass. Even the best rhythm guitar player with the best backup runs in the world would be hard-pressed to make banjo, fiddle, and mandolin sound like much on his/her own. I'd much rather play with a good bass player and a crummy guitarist than with the world's finest guitarist and a lousy bass player.

Many rural string bands played without a bass but the standup bass (aka the "bass fiddle," the "old dog house") was used as a matter of course in the jazz bands Bill Monroe heard in the big cities in the 1920s and '30s. For the musically educated, the instrument we are speaking of is officially known as the three-quarter bass to differentiate it from the larger size symphony orchestra instrument. Bill Monroe knew he needed one in his ensemble. There was going to be too much going on musically with singing and solos not to have a solid underpinning to the whole proceedings. Interestingly, the Kentuckians—Bill Monroe's short-lived and unrecorded pre-Blue Grass Boys ensemble—had no bass but did have a jug player, more proof that Monroe knew his new style of music might have a surging upbeat but it would dance on the foundation of a serious downbeat.

If you're looking to take up a bluegrass instrument but you despair at the oceans of experienced fiddlers and banjo pickers everywhere, consider learning the bass. You'll need to develop some hand strength and it's a good idea to protect your plucking fingers with athletic tape for a while.

The electric guitar–style bass has gotten widespread use by contemporary-style bluegrass bands or those with a country and western-influenced sound; it seems to complement their music. (Personal opinion—Electric basses don't have the string-rebounding effect you feel playing bass fiddles, plus it's not unusual to encounter rock bassists trying to get into bluegrass who equate sweat with speed. That's why it's not unusual to find electric bass players playing real hard trying to go fast. In the process, they drag down the crisp, surging tempos that an experienced banjo or mandolin player will try to establish.)

At any rate, if you learn to thump out a steady beat on a bass in a few keys, you'll suddenly find yourself in greater demand than a fashion model putting an ad in a singles column. Believe me. You should know, however, that bassists in bluegrass bands traditionally have played not only the downbeat but a certain role.

When bluegrass and other country music shows were total entertainment packages, there was plenty of comedy along with the music. Unfortunately for the everlasting image of those stalwart souls who labor in a bluegrass band's engine room, the comedians were usually the bass players. And they were baggy pants comedians. Literally. Oversized trousers held up by outrageous suspenders. Outrageous hillbilly hats. Blacked out teeth. Quizzical expressions.

Maybe this oddity will someday be explained by the discovery of a bizarre genetic anomaly in the DNA of anyone who chooses the bass. Consider this true story. . . .

A good friend of mine approached a famous fiddler to appear

with his band at a local coffee house. My friend was delighted when the great one agreed to sit in for a Saturday night gig. Rehearsal the week before went smashingly. My buddy could taste the artistic triumph ahead.

Then came the night of the performance.

A half hour before show time and no bass player. Twelve minutes and no bass player. Five. Nope, and not even a phone call.

Show time. Arrgh!

Finally—an excruciating ten minutes after the advertised start—prodigal and bass appeared in the doorway. My friend apologized (profusely and for about the fifth time that evening) to their guest artist.

The star responded with a mellowness born of long experience.

"Thar's one in ev'ra band," he drawled philosophically. "And it *ahlways* seems to be the bass player. . . ."

Bluegrass Instruments? No, But Sometimes . . .

AUTOHARP

The caller to a folk club was inquiring about one Bryan Bowers, who was advertised as appearing that night. When told his speciality, she obviously misunderstood.

"What!" she exclaimed. "He plays auto parts?"

Fortunately he doesn't, but what he does play—the autoharp—is mechanically somewhat involved. Basically the autoharp is a zither with chord keys. These keys are spring-loaded and lined underneath with cut felt. Whichever strings aren't touched and dampened by the felt are free to vibrate when struck, so obviously the felt is precut to create a different chord per key. Autoharps were popular parlor instruments in the late nineteenth century, usually laid flat upon a table and strummed with a plectrum for accompaniment while the player sang.

Obviously it wasn't too long before more adventurous musicians started picking up the autoharp—literally. Cradling it in their arms, they could stand next to guitarists and fiddlers. By using fingerpicks and selecting low, middle, or high strings to strike, musicians could play melodies.

The country/folk performer who did the most to popularize the autoharp was Maybelle Carter of the immortal Carter Family of Virginia. Besides her backup work behind the vocals, her instrumental showpiece "Victory Rag" inspired many to give this zinging zither a try.

Although the Carter Family had a huge influence on bluegrass repertoire and rhythm guitar styles, the autoharp has been used by few bluegrass or mountain string band ensembles. Notable exceptions include the autoharp stylings of Stoneman Family patriarch Ernest "Pop" Stoneman and Mike Seeger's revival of the instrument for that old-time music revival group the New Lost City Ramblers. And there is enough interest in the instrument to include an autoharp division at the prestigious Winfield, Kansas, folk and bluegrass contest.

As mentioned earlier, Bryan Bowers has been a popular autoharp exponent for years, often recording in a bluegrass context. A new up-and-comer is Karen Mueller, who adds a crispness to her playing that helps the instrument blend well with the banjo.

Bryan Bowers. *For You,* **Flying Fish 524 (with the Seldom Scene)**
Bill Clifton. *Autoharp Centennial Celebration,* **Elf 101**
Karen Mueller. *Clarity,* **Streamline Productions SL103CD**
Various artists. *Winfield Winners,* **WW 1001**

HAMMERED DULCIMER

If the autoharp is a zither with keys, the hammered dulcimer is a miniature piano without keys and only two hammers; and you hold them, striking the strings like sounding the keys on a xylophone. (Some hammered dulcimer virtuosos get fancy and play duets on one instrument, giving a four-hammer effect.) The instrument is believed to have originated in the Middle East, perhaps in Persia (modern-day Iran). Perhaps the Abyssian maid playing on her dulcimer in Samuel Taylor Coleridge's poem

"Kubla Khan" was using one of the hammered variety. The shimmering, silvery sound of this lovely instrument would sure have been appropriate to Coleridge's psychedelic visions.

The instrument is ideally suited to fiddle tunes and other lively instrumentals. Walt Michael, while with Bottle Hill, introduced it to national folk music audiences. His more recent work with his own ensemble provides fine examples of the instrument in a band context. Not many of the records listed are bluegrass, but many have an old-timey sound that the hammered dulcimer complements beautifully.

John McCutcheon (with Paul Van Arsdale). *Barefoot Boy with Boots On,* **Fro 021**

Metamora. *The Great Road,* **Sugar Hill, 1134**

Walt Michael. *Stepstone,* **Flying Fish 480**

Bill Spence and Fennig's All-Stars. *The Hammered Dulcimer,* **Fro 302**

Trapezoid. *Now and Then,* **Flying Fish 239**

HARMONICA

I'm sorry to report that the venerable mouth organ, which has had a distinguished history in blues, rock, pop, and even hillbilly music, is considered by some bluegrassers to be an ill wind instrument that nobody blows good.

One reason is that the sound of reeds doesn't always blend well with the sound of acoustic strings, especially at high tempos emphasizing the offbeat. (Harmonica played for the downbeat blues or rock-n-roll is an entirely different matter.) There's also a quite understandable prejudice against harmonica players in bluegrass: Blowers who bring their Hohners to festivals and jump into jam sessions rarely know the bluegrass repertoire and seem to think they're country music's answer to Paul Butterfield. They wail away in obnoxious improvisations and never quit, not quite getting the point that all the other melody instruments wait their turns to solo.

But harmonica has blown through the bluegrass in some notable ways. Earl Taylor, the midwestern bluegrass stalwart, doubled on harmonica and mandolin while touring as a Foggy Mountain Boy in the 1960s, with primo Nashville-session harmonica player Charlie McCoy frequently in the studio with Flatt and Scruggs at the end of their career.

While Bela Fleck's jazz-'grass-rock fusion band the Flecktones was exploring new territory in bluegrass-inspired fusion, Howard Levy forged a new technique on the harmonica: overblowing, in which the reeds were blown so hard that they created pitches and overtones beyond those originally intended—or (like Fleck's accomplishments on the banjo) beyond what anyone ever imagined.

On the Nitty Gritty Dirt Band's now legendary *Will the Circle Be Unbroken* album [Capitol 46589], the harmonica played duet and unison solos along with the fiddle. The results were quite nice. And George Thacker has recorded *Bluegrass Harmonica* [Thacker 1], which contains "Rocky Top," Cripple Creek," "Orange Blossom Special," and other standards to which he clearly knows the melodies giving them fine interpretations.

ACCORDION

Before you crack jokes about "Lady of Spain," know that Bill Monroe's beloved redhaired mother played, in addition to the fiddle, the accordion. The instrument was a solid part of the 1942 Blue Grass Boys with accordionist Sally Forrester (wife of fiddle great Howdy Forrester) becoming one of the few Blue Grass Girls in history. Her vamping seventh chords at the end of transitional lines became a part of such classics as the 1942 recording of "Rocky Road Blues."

Although the accordion may never rise to the challenge of keeping up with a blazing version of "Bugle Call Rag," there may be hope for the old box yet: Scots-Irish folk music uses accordion to fine effect and New England contra dance bands (which play for the line dance equivalent of southern square dancing) routinely use another keyboard instrument, the piano, to provide a rhythm foundation.

APPENDIX ONE
Bluegrass Roots and Branches

[The star] had to be from humble beginnings, just like the audience. . . . The star had to sing about those beginnings and the other things he had shared with people from those beginnings. . . .

—Pop music critic Chet Flippo on country music

Several forms of traditional-style country music have played vital roles in the development of bluegrass. As you get deeper into bluegrass, you're sure to hear about these other kinds of music and the performers who made them great.

Listen to them. But don't worry, it won't be a dry academic exercise. Some of the liveliest and most moving music America has ever produced is waiting for you.

Jimmie Rodgers and the Carter Family

In the summer of 1927, Ralph Peer, a representative of Okeh Records (who would one day found the major Peer Southern music publishing house) set up his recording equipment at a hotel in Bristol, Tennessee, and put out announcements that he was preparing to record talented musicians.

He got more than he could have imagined.

On August 1 and 2, he recorded for the first time the Carter Family of Virginia, a talented trio specializing in lovely old ballads. On August 4, he recorded Jimmie Rodgers, a white railroad worker from Mississippi who specialized in Negro blues.

What Peer had done for country music was basically the equivalent of a rock-n-roll producer discovering both the Beatles and Elvis, within two days of each other.

Jimmie Charles Rodgers, the son of a railroad foreman, absorbed black music and then developed his own style that featured "blue" yodeling. With the possible exception of Enrico Caruso, Jimmie Rodgers was the first superstar of the modern recording industry and certainly the first major popular music vocalist.

Bill Monroe was obviously influenced by Jimmie Rodgers as witness his arrangement of "Muleskinner Blues." Country-and-western vocalists as seemingly diverse as Gene Autry and Ernest Tubb patterned themselves in their early years directly after the Yodeling Brakeman. Listen today to virtually any country-and-western male vocalist: under his individual vocal landscape is the fertile loam of Hank Williams, supported by the bedrock of Jimmie Rodgers.

Alvin P. Carter, better known as A. P. Carter, was a salesman with a love of music who married Sara Dougherty, an accomplished singer. They began performing songs in their local area and were soon joined by Maybelle Addington Carter (A.P.'s sister-in-law). Both women played autoharp and guitar and harmonized sweetly, while A.P. added his rich baritone/bass. They had a vast repertoire of old folk songs: "Wildwood Flower," "Keep On the Sunny Side," and "Will the Circle Be Unbroken" were just a few they collected, arranged, and popularized.

They performed them beautifully but also with high professionalism. Such was their influence that today there is probably no living bluegrass, country, or folk musician who doesn't use a song, harmony style, or rhythm-guitar technique borrowed from this Virginia trio.

The Carter Family. *Clinch Mountain Treasures,* **County 112**
————. *Anchored in Love,* **Rounder 1064**

————. *My Clinch Mountain Home,* **Rounder 1065**
Jimmie Rodgers. *First Sessions,* **Rounder 1056**
————. *The Early Years,* **Rounder 1057**

Bluegrass Brothers

Sure, duet harmonies are common in folk music. But bluegrass duets are typically tight and have a real edge to them. Why? Maybe because of the bluegrass brothers.

Brother duet acts (usually with guitar and mandolin accompaniment) were immensely popular in the early days of country music. The Monroe Brothers were of course the kings (for recommended listening, see below). But there were others, sometimes not even brothers but men possessed of a sound like blood relations.

Some of the best of these include the Bailes Brothers (*Grand Ole Opry and More,* White Dove 1054); the Bailey Brothers (*Just as the Sun Went Down,* Rounder 0056); and the wonderful Blue Sky Boys (Bill and Earl Bolick), who achieved a new moment of acclaim in 1973 when their music was used by director Peter Bogdanovich in the movie *Paper Moon* (*In Concert, 1964,* Rounder 11536; *On Radio,* County 0120 and 0121); and an act admired by Doc Watson and others, the Delmore Brothers (*Sandy Mountain Blues,* County 110).

Far from being a quaint (and dead) sound, the genre is being used to great effect by Josh Crowe and David McLaughlin (*Going Back,* Rounder 0314); the Case Brothers (*Old Time Country Duets with Guitar and Mandolin,* Case Brothers 001); Rabbit in a Log—Skip Gorman and Rick Starkey, taking their name from a popular Monroe Brothers ditty—(*Late Last Night,* Marimac 9602); the Whitstein Brothers (*Old Time Duets,* Rounder 0264); and others.

Credit for really resurrecting the format must go to Ricky Skaggs and Tony Rice (with their acclaimed *Skaggs and Rice,* Sugar Hill 3711). Rice has followed up with Norman Blake (*Norman Blake and Tony Rice,* Rounder 0233). Two other veterans, Bill Clifton and Jimmy Gaudreau, have recently added their talents to the form (*River of Memories,* Elf Records 103), as have new-comers Mike Compton and David Grier (*Climbing the Walls,* Rounder 0280).

Don't overlook the excellent male/female duets, particularly Delia Bell and Bill Grant (*A Few Dollars More,* Rounder 0217). Also very satisfying are the recordings of Jody Stecher and Kate Brislin (*Blue Lightning,* Rounder 0284), Barry and Holly Tashian (*Ready for Love,* Rounder 0302), and Bob and Dana Kogut (*Heart of the Mountains,* Pinecastle 1016).

Recording duets in the context of small, three- or four-piece bands are some very popular husband/wife and brother/sister acts. Especially if you like modern folk music or light western swing, you're sure to enjoy Phil and Gaye Johnson (*Live: Mountain Flower/The Lost Broadcast,* Aster-Etcetera 2001/2002), Tim and Mollie O'Brien (*Away Out on the Mountain,* Sugar Hill 3825), or Robin and Linda Williams (*Turn Toward Tomorrow,* Sugar Hill 1040).

The primo country music duet act—without question—was the Louvin Brothers. The Louvins were not only superb singers but also wrote songs of deep emotional impact. One masterpiece is "When I Stop Dreaming," with its poetic allusions to a spurned lover forced to exist like a neglected flower in a garden of undying pain. "Cash on the Barrelhead," although light in tone, has some rough things to say about modern life. Ira, a tormented genius and a hugely underrated mandolinist, died in a car crash in 1964, but the Louvins' music survives in the person of Charlie, who still appears on the Grand Ole Opry. (Charlie Louvin recently recorded in a bluegrass context: *Bluegrass Style,* NPB 029).

The Louvin Brothers' music is collected in *Radio Favorites 1951–1957* (Country Music Foundation 009), and the mega-collection of virtually their entire studio output, *Close Harmony* (Bear Family 15561).

Ira Louvin received the ultimate posthumous compliment from Bill Monroe. When asked to name the greatest tenor singer in country music, Monroe replied, "Ain't but two of us, and Ira's dead."

Music by the Monroe Brothers includes:

Monroe Brothers (Bill and Charlie). *Feast Here Tonight,* **RCA Bluebird AMX2-5510 (definitive collection)**

Birch Monroe. *Brother Birch Monroe Plays Old Time Fiddle Favorites,* **Atteiram 1516**

Charlie Monroe. *Charlie Monroe's Boys: The Early Years (1938–39),* **Old Homestead 133**

Bluegrass Cousins

> I can see fiddling around with a banjo, but how do you banjo around with a fiddle?
>
> **—Duncan Purney, music critic**

As numerous civil wars have proven, conflict between relatives can be particularly nasty. There hasn't been any outright warfare between bluegrass and old-time music, but newcomers who naively lump the two together are often surprised to learn that relations between these string band country cousins is some-times downright acrimonious.

Some old-time players consider bluegrass to be a cheap, flashy, modern ripoff of beautiful old mountain music, in which faster is equated with better. Some bluegrass players consider old-time music to be a simplistic free-for-all devoid of even the most basic appreciation of harmony and improvisation, in which endless and mindless unison playing is equated with soulful intensity.

As many a true word has been said in jest, the following two jokes, which have made the rounds of the folk music scene, are offered by way of illustration:

Old-time musician's joke: A violin virtuoso with no further heights to scale in classical music became enamored of old-time music. But his brain was so crammed with music theory that he couldn't truly play the fiddle. So he insisted on having a partial lobotomy.

After the operation, his surgeon met with the violinist's family and he looked distinctly uncomfortable. "Is he all right?" they asked.

"Oh yes," said the surgeon. "In fact, he's awake and playing the fiddle."

"Then whatever is the matter, doctor?"

"I think I took out too much of his brain," the surgeon replied. "He's playing bluegrass."

Bluegrass musician's joke: What's the difference between an old-time band playing a tune during an old-time music festival jam session and an Uzi submachine gun?

Answer: The Uzi quits after 40 rounds.

Between these extremes is a middle ground of mutual appreciation—plus music that is not exactly bluegrass but that shares a lot of the same sensibilities. I call them "cousins" to bluegrass and they're a joy.

For example, many old-time string bands widened the wagon roads for the bluegrass that was to follow, notably Charlie Poole and the North Carolina Ramblers (*Old Time Songs*, Columbia 3501), Gid Tanner and the Skillet Lickers (*The Skillet Lickers Volumes 1 & 2*, County 506 & 526), and Fiddlin' Arthur Smith and His Dixieliners (*Fiddlin' Arthur Smith and His Dixieliners, Volumes 1 & 2*, County 546 & 547).

Among the old-time performers contemporary with bluegrass and/or close to it were Wade Mainer (*Carolina Mule*, Old Homestead 90207), the venerable J. E. Mainer and the Mountaineers (*Bluegrass Favorites*, Rural Rhythm 198), Roy Hall and His Blue Ridge Entertainers (*Roy Hall and His Blue Ridge Entertainers*, County 406), Jim Greer and the Mac-O-Chee Valley Folks (*Old Time Country Favorites*, Rural Rhythm 161), and Clint Howard—a former Doc Watson accompanist—and the Blueridge Mountain Boys (*Way Down in My Cabin Home*, Old Homestead 90177).

Molly O'Day and the Cumberland County Folks (*Molly O'Day and the Cumberland County Folks*, Bear Family Records 15565) and Wilma Lee, Stoney Cooper, and the Clinch Mountain Clan (*Early Recordings*, County 103) were country bands with many bluegrass admirers. An extremely important bluegrass "country cousin" was Roy Acuff, "The King of Country Music" and one of the major stars of the Grand Ole Opry. Acuff kept his ensemble close to its acoustic country string band roots and provided many songs for the bluegrass repertoire (*The Essential Roy Acuff, 1936–1949*, Columbia/Legacy 48956).

Pre-bluegrass rural string band music was a natural for the folk song craze of the 1950s and '60s. The New Lost City Ramblers (John Cohen, Mike Seeger, and Tom Paley, later replaced by Tracy Schwartz) led a revival of interest in the form. They were so serious about authenticity that they were good-naturedly accused of copying old recordings right down to the mistakes (*The Early Years, 1958–1962*, Smithsonian/Folkways 40036; also listen to Mike Seeger, *Old Time Country Music*, Rounder 0278).

The New Lost City Ramblers, the Plank Road String Band, and other old-time revival bands are found on the well-titled *Young Fogies* (Rounder 0319). Other modern groups that make the old sounds come alive are Mac Benford and the Woodshed All-Stars (*1st 1/2C*, Marimac 9047), Norman and Nancy Blake and the Rising Fawn String Band (*Natasha's Waltz*, Rounder 11530), and Allan "Mac" McHale and the Old-Time Radio Gang (*New River Train*, Folk Era 1048).

Melding the best of bluegrass, old-time, and contemporary folk music is Walt Michael and Company. Michael's silvery hammered dulcimer playing adds a lovely extra dimension to their recordings (*The Good Old Way*, Fro 033). The Red Clay Ramblers (*Rambler*, Sugar Hill 3798) defy analysis and categorization.

Finally, a real noteworthy bluegrass cousin was actually Bill Monroe's brother and former duet partner, Charlie. He never joined the Grand Ole Opry and is hence less remembered today as a major country music figure. But Charlie Monroe and the Kentucky Partners were immensely popular in the South in the 1940s and early '50s, and their music could be as nearly as lively as Bill's and certainly more heartwarming.

Charlie had a glad voice that he used well. The songs he made famous promoted frolicsome fun ("That's What I Like About You"), made tender pleas ("It's Only A Phonograph Record"), recorded the anxieties of war and parting ("I'm Coming Back but I Don't Know When"), or told eternal tales of tragedy ("Down in the Willow Garden"). Charlie Monroe died in 1974 but he will still greet you with a musical grin if you seek him out (*Songs He Made Famous*, Old Homestead 304; *Tally Ho!*, Starday 484-498).

APPENDIX TWO

Resources

Histories of Bluegrass and Related Country/Folk Musics

The overwhelming majority of bluegrass books are instructional manuals—how to play banjo, fiddle, mandolin, dobro, guitar, bass, even how to sing. For reasons of space, these are not listed here. Don't worry, it's easy to find them. Pick up a bluegrass magazine or visit a music vendor at any bluegrass or folk festival.

There are worthwhile books on the history of the music. Like jazz, bluegrass and related traditional-style country musics have been blessed with numerous outstanding writer/scholars whose work is both well-researched and highly readable.

Because you've gotten this far, you'll want to find them. And because I've gotten this far, I want to list them because I'm hugely indebted to the work of their authors. Find these works at your local bookstore, through major mail order record companies (who often have them in stock), or at your local library. (If a book isn't on the shelf, ask the librarian about a title search and inter-library loan.)

The definitive work to date is *Bluegrass: A History* by Neil V. Rosenberg (University of Illinois Press, 1985). Rosenberg, one of the leading chroniclers of bluegrass, examines the music through each significant period of its development from its rural string

215

band roots through the impact of newgrass. The folk song boom, which gave bluegrass a tremendous boost, is examined in the collection *Transforming Tradition: Folk Music Revivals Examined,* (University of Illinois Press, 1993). Rosenberg, who edited this book, has also written detailed booklets accompanying some of the major reissues of bluegrass on compact disc.

In *Bluegrass* (Hawthorne Books, 1975), Bob Artis does an excellent job of giving a popular but still historically rich treatment to the bands and trends covered in more scholarly detail by Rosenberg. *Bluegrass Breakdown: The Making of the Old Southern Sound,* by Robert Cantwell (University of Illinois Press, 1984), is an insightful analysis of how mountain music was reinvented by Bill Monroe and other southerners who had moved to big cities in search of work in the 1920s and 1930s.

Valuable information on southern music, including bluegrass and its roots, is found in the writings of Bill C. Malone: *Country Music USA: A Fifty-Year History* (University of Texas Press, 1968) is an exceptional study of the music as a cultural force and an industry; its international importance is documented in *Southern Music—American Music* (University of Kentucky Press, 1979); and the more recent *Singing Cowboys and Musical Mountaineers: Southern Culture and the Roots of Country Music* (University of Georgia Press, 1993) goes further into the hillbilly and western sounds that have been "daddies" and "cousins" to bluegrass.

The late Ralph Rinzler, a folklorist and Smithsonian official, played a crucial role in the music's history when he revitalized Monroe's career in the 1960s by championing his music to national audiences during the folk music revival. (Rinzler also discovered Doc Watson, recorded numerous mountain musicians, and assisted country music promoter Carlton Haney in developing the bluegrass festival format that we know today.) Rinzler's numerous articles and record/CD liner notes contain some of the best writing ever done about Monroe and bluegrass. The booklets that accompany *Bill Monroe and the Blue Grass Boys off the Record* (Smithsonian/Folkways 40063) and Bill Monroe with Doc Watson, *Live Duet Recordings,* Smithsonian/Folkways 40064) are particularly recommended. Also highly valuable is Rinzler's chapter on Monroe in *Stars of Country Music: Uncle Dave Macon to Johnny Rodriguez,* Bill C. Malone and Judith McCulloh editors (University of Illinois Press, 1975).

As of this writing, a scholarly biography of Bill Monroe has not appeared. Ralph Rinzler once told me he was assisting Monroe on some autobiographical writings, but to date this material has not become public. In the meantime a succinct and often compelling work is Jim Rooney's *Bossmen: Bill Monroe and Muddy Waters.* This outstanding dual biography of the father of bluegrass and the master of the blues includes lengthy observations by Monroe about his life and career (Dial Press, 1971 reissued as a paperback by Da Capo Press, 1991). Rooney and Eric von Schmidt chronicle New England bluegrass in the course of their entertaining history of the Boston/Cambridge folk music scene *Baby, Let Me Follow You Down* (Anchor Books, 1979, reissued by University of Massachusetts Press, 1994).

There's more on bluegrass from the wheelhoss's mouth in Alanna Nash's extended interview with Bill Monroe in *Behind Closed Doors: Talking with the Legends of Country Music* (Alfred A. Knopf, 1988). Ralph Stanley is viewed from numerous perspectives in *Traveling the High Way Home: Ralph Stanley and the World of Traditional Bluegrass Music* by John Wright (University of Illinois Press, 1993). Ivan M. Tribe, a longtime bluegrass historian, has written the history of one famous bluegrass clan in *The Stonemans: An Appalachian Family and the Music That Shaped Their Lives* (University of Illinois Press, 1993). Information from sixty-eight leading banjo players, eighteen in-depth interviews with five-string stars (and closeup photos of their picking hands!), tablatures, and discographies, plus a chat with Bill Monroe (who is not a banjo player but who has hired enough of them and thus qualifies as an expert) make up the monumental *Masters of the 5-String Banjo* by Tony Trischka and Pete Wernick (Oak Publications, 1988).

The list of lovingly written biographies of country and mountain music "cousins" to bluegrass is long, so here are just some of the best.

Janette Carter tells the story of her kin, the famous Carter Family, and the humble world from which they came in *Living with Memories* (Center for Cultural Resources, 1983). Jimmie Rodgers is the subject of the excellent study and discography *Jimmie Rodgers*, by Nolan Porterfield (University of Illinois Press, 1979), and of the 1935 first-person account *My Husband, Jimmie Rodgers*, by Carrie Rodgers (reprinted by the Country Music Foundation Press, 1975). *Truth Is Stranger Than Publicity*, the autobiography of Alton Delmore (Country Music Foundation Press, 1977), is fascinating not only because of Alton's role as one of the Delmore Brothers but for his insider's view of the early country music business. The stories of other legendary old-timey musicians are presented (along with extensive discographies) in *Bradley Kincaid: Radio's Kentucky's Mountain Boy* by Loyal Jones (Berea College, 1980) and *Rambling Blues: The Life and Songs of Charlie Poole* by C. Kinney Rorrer (Old Time Music, 1985).

Regions of the American South have also had their musical biographies: *Mountaineer Jamboree* (University of Illinois Press, 1985) by Ivan M. Tribe documents country music in West Virginia, including the legendary WWVA Jamboree radio show; *Tennessee Traditional Singers,* edited by Thomas G. Burton (University of Tennessee Press, 1981), features studies of blues and old-timey musicians Tom Ashley, Sam McGee, and Bukka White; *Tennessee Strings* by Charles K. Wolfe (University of Tennessee Press, 1977) covers rural music and includes a chapter on the WSM Grand Ole Opry; *Kentucky Country,* also by Wolfe (University Press of Kentucky, 1982), chronicles music in the Bluegrass state from frontier settlers through Bill Monroe to coal miner's daughter/country star Loretta Lynn.

Other books on bluegrass include *Old as the Hills: The Story of Bluegrass* by Steven D. Price (Viking, 1975); *Grass Roots: An Illustrated History of Bluegrass and Mountain Music* by Fred Hill (Academy Books, 1980); and *The Big Book of Bluegrass* (Morrow, 1984), a collection of interviews and features from the old *Frets* magazine edited by Marilyn Kochman.

There have been additional discographies of individual performers such as Neil Rosenberg's *Bill Monroe and His Blue Grass Boys: An Illustrated Discography* (Country Music Foundation Press, 1974; no longer in print, but as of this writing photocopies are available from the CMF in Nashville). *The Stanley Brothers: A Preliminary Discography* has been published privately by Gary B. Reid and *Bluegrass LP Issues, 1957–1990,* a broad discography, was published in Australia by John Boothroyd in 1990. Perhaps the best sources these days for discographies and recording session information on any band are the detailed booklets included in major reissues on compact disc. Happy reading!

Magazines and Newsletters

Magazines about bluegrass and old-time country music are your best source for keeping current on the music and/or learning more about its wonderful past. Besides features on artists old and new, most have reviews, announcements of upcoming festivals and concerts, even listings of clubs and radio shows in the United States and overseas. I'd particularly recommend them as up-to-date sources for purchasing recordings, instructional books and tapes, instruments, strings, and accessories.

This is a current list, but remember magazines do go out of business. I have not included scholarly journals in this listing, but there are several that publish academic papers on bluegrass and old-time country music.

Acoustic Guitar Newsletter
P.O. Box 28
Glenford OH 43739

Acoustic Musician
P.O. Box 1349
New Market, VA 22844-1349
703-740-4005

Banjo Newsletter
P.O. Box 3418
Annapolis, MD 21403
800-759-7425 or 410-263-6503

Bluegrass Canada
#1-231 Victoria Street
Kamloops, British Columbia, Canada V2C 2A1

Bluegrass Unlimited
Box 111
Broad Run, VA 22104
800-BLU-GRAS or 703-349-8181

Fiddler Magazine
P.O. Box 125
Los Altos, CA 94022

The Mandocrucian's Digest
P.O. Box 3585
Winchester, VA 22604

Organizations

There are numerous regional bluegrass clubs in the United States, Canada, Europe, Asia, and Australia/New Zealand that advertise from time to time in bluegrass and folk publications or the Arts and Leisure listings of local newspapers. The two major U.S. national organizations offer various "clearinghouse" information services, hold conventions, and present annual awards for most popular artists. They are:

International Bluegrass Music Association (IBMA)
207 East Second St.
Owensboro, KY 42302
502-684-9025

Society for the Preservation of Bluegrass Music in America
(SPBMGA)
P.O. Box 271
Kirksville, MO 63501
816-665-7172

These organizations can sometimes help you find good bluegrass on the airwaves. Or you can contact:

American Bluegrass Network, the ABN Group
5108 South Orange Avenue
Orlando, FL 32809
407-856-0245

Bluegrass Radio Network
P.O. Box 542
Pendleton, OR
503-278-1214

Where to Find Bluegrass Records

One of the best and most satisfying sources for bluegrass recordings is festivals and shows. Hearkening back to the days when performers toured the southern hills and sold records out of the trunks of their cars, bluegrass bands sell their recordings direct to fans at their shows. It's a win-win situation: No middle-person; you get the recording you want plus an autograph (imagine the collector's value, too); the musicians pay for fuel, food, and motel rooms with the record proceeds and can save their appearance monies.

It should be stressed that major bluegrass-oriented labels will sell direct to you, the consumer, and are often pleased to send you a catalog of their current offerings. *Bluegrass Unlimited* and some other periodicals list the appropriate recording companies at the end of their reviews, so you can contact the issuer directly—an extremely helpful practice when the recording in question is self-produced or by an overseas band.

But if you can't wait to hear some good bluegrass, the good news is that more and more mainstream tape and CD stores have a separate bluegrass section. A quick perusal under individual artists' names and through the folk and country sections will often reveal other bluegrass recordings ready for purchase.

Used record shops—now proliferating in cities and college towns—are also excellent places to locate hard-to-find albums, and many have a separate bluegrass bin. (Suggestion: bluegrass discs are often misfiled by shop personnel under the folk and country-and-western headings, so search there too.)

The even better news is that the mail order companies listed below specialize in bluegrass and old-time music titles, and have reputations for good selection, reliability, and fairly fast turnaround. Again, major record producers have their own catalogs but here I've listed only companies that sell a range of labels.

Things have certainly changed since the 1960s, when us Yankees were lucky to find anything other than Flatt and Scruggs in the stores. I first went to college in a little town in southern Pennsylvania and was joyously amazed to walk into a local music shop and find Jimmy Martin, Jim and Jesse, and Bill Monroe albums in the stacks, all shiny and new and just waiting to go back to my dorm room with me. (Many did.) Dave Freeman, who ran County Sales in the 1960s from an apartment in Manhattan (and still had plenty of room for inventory) now receives more records for consideration every few weeks than he received in his entire first year of business. Needless to say, he's now in Virginia and owns a warehouse.

If you're just getting into bluegrass, you've come at the right time.

Bell Mountain Music
P.O. Box 288
Hiawassee, GA 30546
706-896-5016

County Sales
Box 191
Floyd, VA 24901
703-745-2001

DaSBro Enterprise
2760 Grand Concourse, Dept. B
Bronx, NY 10458
800-786-6035

Don's Recycled Records
P.O. Box 1353
Park Ridge, IL 60068

Elderly Instruments
1100 N. Washington
P.O. Box 14210
Lansing, MI 48906
517-372-7890

Uncle Jim O'Neal
Box A
Arcadia, CA 91066-8001

Voyager Recordings and Publications
424 35th Avenue
Seattle, WA 98122

The above companies have many out-of-print recordings on their shelves, in limited quantities but still in stock. Remember, it never hurts to ask. But if your search for a special old disc becomes more challenging than the quest for the Holy Grail, try the following specialists in rare bluegrass and old-time country music records:

Gary Edwards
Spinners Records
635 E. Olive
Fresno, CA 93728

Charlie James
Box 62
Pierrefonds, Quebec, Canada H9H 4K8

John Morris
Old Homestead Records
P.O. Box 100
Brighton, MI 48116

Bill Vernon
P.O. Box 472
Rocky Mount, VA 24151

Learning at the Electronic Knee: Audio and Video Cassette Instruction

The same thing that can be said about the relative ease of finding bluegrass recordings can be said about finding recorded instruction. As mentioned in the introduction, I haven't included instructional materials in recommended/representative listening lists in each chapter. But here's where to start. Checking out their ads in the bluegrass publications is extremely useful: You may be delighted to find that your favorite performer has a teaching tape on the market.

The following are main producers and/or suppliers of a variety of instructional programs (different instruments, different instrumental styles, singing and harmony styles, etc.), usually featuring major artists.

Homespun Video
Box 694B
Woodstock, NY 12498
800-338-2737

The Murphy Method
P.O. Box 2498A
Winchester, VA 22604
800-227-2357

Ridge Runner Home Lessons
84 York Creek Drive
Driftwood, TX 78619
800-FRET-PRO or 512-847-8605

Texas Music and Video
P.O. Box 8101
Levelland, TX 79338
800-874-8384

Workshop Records
P.O. Box 49507
Austin, TX 78765
800-543-6125

And here are some specialists in a particular instrument. There are lots of fine, although little-known, pickers waiting to instruct you but I've limited the following to nationally known recording artists. "Seminar" means providers run one- or multi-day workshops or camps. (These are usually not offered year-round, so inquire early.) Instruction is a rapidly growing field, especially as big-name performers start looking for an alternative to all those weeks each year on the road. So keep scanning bluegrass magazines for the latest offerings.

Band Seminars: Peter Wernick
7930 Oxford Road
Niwot, CO 80503

Banjo: Al Munde's Banjo College
P.O. Box 8240
Levelland, TX 79338

Banjo Seminars: Peter Wernick
7930 Oxford Road
Niwot, CO 80503

Dobro: Boze Music Company
P.O. Box 7402
Shreveport, LA 71137

Fiddle: Benny Sims
318 Sewanee Drive
Johnson City, TN 37604
615-282-1219

Byron Berline, 818-986-3791

Fiddle Seminars: Mark O'Connor Fiddle Camp
P.O. Box 150802
Nashville, TN
615-297-7188

Guitar: Steve Kaufman
P.O. Box 1020
Alcoa, TN 37701
800-FLATPIK or 615-982-3808

Mandolin: Frank Wakefield
P.O. Box 1293
Saratoga Springs, NY 12866

Mandolin Seminars: Butch Baldassari
125 43rd Avenue North
Nashville, TN 37209
615-292-0324

Multi-instructional: Camp Bluegrass
Alan Munde and Joe Carr
South Plains College
Levelland, TX 79336
806-894-9611 or 806-894-4874

APPENDIX THREE

Bluegrass Festivals and How to Thrive at Them

If you're new to bluegrass music and you've gotten this far in the book, you'll want to attend your first bluegrass festival. Omitting some information on festivals for the new bluegrasser would be like leaving out information on the Bayreuth Festival Theater for the aspiring Wagnerian. Here's what to expect.

Basic Survival

It's a rare festival that doesn't sell a single day's admission. (Saturdays often have the best lineups and Sunday mornings traditionally feature bluegrass gospel.) Of course, weekend passes have the cheapest rates.

If you want to stay overnight, you can survive if you have camping skills at least at the level of a Tenderfoot scout.

Get there early and try to find a shady spot. Otherwise, be prepared to arise by 9 A.M. as the sun starts heating up your tent. Crime is pretty low at these things but don't leave instruments or valuables unattended. On the other hand, never ever leave your instrument (or newly purchased records, tapes, and CDs) in the trunk of your car where by noontime it will be cooked.

Be prepared with caps, sunglasses, and sunscreen (for the days), insect repellent (for hot nights), a sweater (for cool nights), and toilet paper (in case the portable johns run out, which happens). Some places have showers but in general, prepare to live with just washing your face and hands. (Of course, this is not a problem if you get a motel room, but book reservations in advance.) Bring a blanket to sit on—one that you don't mind getting dirty. Bring rain gear.

It's cheaper to bring your own food than to feed at the concession stands, but I like to bring food that can be quickly prepared: The time you spend cooking you can't spend picking or listening. Bring a canteen or plastic water bottle and make sure you drink from it through the day so you won't get sick from fluid loss. (This is important; you're going to be outside all day!) Check ahead to see if pets are allowed. (Often they aren't.)

Make sure you have good directions. Check a map well in advance of pulling out of your driveway. Don't be afraid to call and ask the promoter for specific directions. It's more fun to be sitting down at the main stage area on a Friday night than driving around lost in the country with the same cows staring at you every time you drive by.

For the most part, these are family shows. There have been problems in the past involving open drug use, drunks, or visiting motorcycle gangs. But today's festival promoters know they must have family shows or go out of business, so things are generally orderly and mellow. I can't guarantee you'll never have a problem, but picking in the parking lot of a bluegrass festivals at 1 A.M. is much safer than being in the parking lot of a convenience store at the same hour. (Hint: Patronize festivals that advertise "No Drugs, No Alcohol" or at least "No Alcohol in Main Stage Area.")

Leave Your Tape Recorder at Home; Bring Cash or Credit Card

Recording in the main stage area is generally discouraged. In fact, I'm going to discourage it further.

Musicians deserve to be able to sell their own studio recordings. And boy, is this the place to get them! Not only from vendors but usually from the bands themselves who often set up tables of recordings, t-shirts, ball caps, song books, photos, videos, and bumper stickers. Not only can you get an autograph on your souvenir (enhancing its collector's value), but every dollar the musicians make on their goods means one less dollar of their appearance money they have to sacrifice for gas, food, and lodgings. So you're supporting the arts. (No, an Alison Krauss t-shirt is not tax deductible.)

Jam Sessions

Bluegrass is participatory in a way few other musics are. Spontaneous jam sessions by fans occur away from the main stage area (known generically as "parking lot picking," although most of it goes on at campsites). How many chamber quartets have you seen setting up on the grounds of Wolftrap Farm during a weekend of classical music? Wander through the campgrounds, especially after the main stage finale late at night, and you can listen in on some great music. Occasionally, a professional picker may be found playing with some advanced amateurs and you can watch them up close. Bluegrass, like a good campfire, seems to burn more fragrantly and brighter in the open air.

If you're looking to do some picking yourself, here's some jam session etiquette: Try to find a session that is not too far above your abilities. (But not too far below either. You want to improve, after all.) Approach any gathering of musicians as you would a group in conversation at a party. Join in if it seems appropriate but stay out if it seems closed.

How to tell? If there is a tight knot of hot, advanced pickers containing one of each of the usual bluegrass instruments (banjo, mandolin, fiddle, bass, guitar), you might be extraneous. Jam sessions are musical conversations. Don't intrude boorishly and try to dominate them. Give and take.

However, it is perfectly acceptable for beginners to stand off to the side and pick quietly along. If you're just learning and are unsure of your timing, notes, chording, repertoire, etc., this is a great way to learn.

But once you've gained confidence through hours of practice and preparation, find a friendly jam session and dive in as you would dive into a pool and swim. If you drop a note or even blow an entire solo, don't berate yourself. Just keep playing.

Sessions are generally quite friendly. As you move up through the intermediate ranks you may encounter some hotshots who want to establish their musical dominance by outplaying everyone else, especially anyone playing the same instrument as them. In jazz circles, musical encounters with a nasty competitive subtext are known as "cutting sessions." Fortunately, they're rare. Cooperation and a feeling of hail-fellow-well-met (or should I say, "Hi, y'all!") is usually the name of the game. It's a great way to make new friends.

WHAT NOT TO REQUEST AND HOW

For listeners, requests are acceptable. But don't be pushy. Be advised that the following songs and tunes have been massively overplayed. Maybe you just can't get enough of your favorites but the pickers are usually weary of them. (And they are definitely sick of hearing these accompanying insistent shouts):

1. "Foggy Mountain Breakdown" ("Play Bonnie and Clyde!")
2. "The Ballad of Jed Clampett" ("Play the Beverly Hillbillies!")
3. "Dueling Banjos" ("Hey, can you guys do Deliverance?")
4. "Rocky Top" ("Good old Rocky Top Tennessee!!")
5. "Glendale Train" ("Somebody robbed the Glendale train!")
6. "Orange Blossom Special" ("Play that fast fiddle one!")

With this final piece of vital information, you've now had a full introduction to bluegrass.

INDEX

Bluegrass: An Informal Guide emphasizes musicians and musical styles, so that's mostly what you'll find indexed. There simply wasn't room to list song and album titles nor every person of historical importance. Similarly, only artists discussed in the text are listed below (although some additional names appear in the recommended listening sections at the end of each chapter).

ABOUT THE AUTHOR

Richard D. Smith was "country when country wasn't cool," having started playing bluegrass 30 years ago on a rural route in central New Jersey. He has played mandolin with several semi-professional bands. As a journalist and researcher, he contributes to numerous national and regional publications. For the past 15 years he has been a staff writer and record reviewer for *Bluegrass Unlimited* magazine. He currently lives in Rocky Hill, New Jersey.

DISCARDED